THE ULTIMATE MEDITERRANEAN DIET COOKBOOK

2000 Days Of Easy Breakfast, Lunch, and Dinner Cooking Recipes for Busy Beginners on Deliciously Healthy Eating and Effortless Weight Management

SCARLETT WATERS

TABLE OF CONTENTS

Introduction

In a world filled with countless diet trends promising quick fixes and miraculous results, the Mediterranean diet stands out as a beacon of wholesome, sustainable eating. Originating from the culinary traditions of the Mediterranean region, this diet has garnered widespread attention for its emphasis on fresh, whole foods and its potential to promote longevity and well-being.

THE MEDITERRANEAN DIET: WHAT KIND OF DIET IS IT?

At its core, the Mediterranean diet is more than just a list of foods to eat; it's a lifestyle centered around the principles of balance, moderation, and enjoyment. Unlike restrictive fad diets, this approach encourages a diverse array of nutrient-rich foods, drawing inspiration from the traditional eating patterns of countries like Greece, Italy, and Spain.

THE KEY CONCEPTS OF MEDITERRANEAN DIET

Central to the Mediterranean diet are plant-based foods such as fruits, vegetables, whole grains, nuts, and legumes. These form the foundation of meals, providing essential vitamins, minerals, and fiber while minimizing the consumption of processed foods and added sugars. Olive oil, a staple fat in this diet, is celebrated for its heart-healthy monounsaturated fats and antioxidant properties. Moderate consumption of fish, poultry, and dairy products, particularly yogurt and cheese, is also encouraged. Red meat is enjoyed sparingly, typically reserved for special occasions. Herbs, spices, and garlic add flavor to dishes, reducing the need for excessive salt and enhancing the culinary experience.

GUIDELINE FOR SUCCESS ON MEDITERRANEAN DIET

Adopting the Mediterranean diet is not about strict rules or deprivation but rather about embracing a holistic approach to eating. To succeed on this journey, focus on incorporating a variety of colorful, whole foods into your meals. Prioritize seasonal produce, experiment with different grains and legumes, and aim for a balance between different food groups.

Portion control and mindful eating are key components of the Mediterranean lifestyle. Listen to your body's hunger and fullness cues, savor each bite, and cultivate a deeper appreciation for the flavors and textures of your food. Additionally, regular physical activity complements the diet, contributing to overall health and well-being.

HEALTH BENEFITS OF MEDITERRANEAN DIET

Research has consistently shown that adhering to the Mediterranean diet is associated with numerous health benefits. From reducing the risk of chronic diseases such as heart disease, diabetes, and certain cancers to promoting weight management and cognitive function, the evidence is compelling. The abundance of fruits, vegetables, and whole grains provides essential nutrients and antioxidants that support immune function and reduce inflammation. The inclusion of healthy fats from sources like olive oil and fatty fish helps maintain optimal cholesterol levels and protects against cardiovascular disease. Moreover, the emphasis on social eating and enjoyment fosters a positive relationship with food and enhances overall quality of life.

THE MEDITERRANEAN DIET'S ESSENTIAL INGREDIENTS AND KITCHEN UTENSILS

Stocking your kitchen with the right ingredients and utensils can make embracing the Mediterranean diet both convenient and enjoyable. Essential pantry items include extra virgin olive oil, whole grains such as quinoa and bulgur, canned beans and tomatoes, nuts and seeds, and a variety of herbs and spices.

In terms of kitchen utensils, invest in quality olive oil pourers, a set of sharp knives for chopping fruits and vegetables, a sturdy cutting board, and versatile cookware like a cast-iron skillet and a non-stick sauté pan. A citrus juicer, garlic press, and mortar and pestle can also come in handy for preparing flavorful dressings and sauces.

In conclusion, the Mediterranean diet offers a time-tested approach to eating that prioritizes health, flavor, and sustainability. By embracing its principles and incorporating its delicious and nutritious foods into your daily life, you can embark on a journey towards improved well-being and longevity. So, let's savor the vibrant flavors of the Mediterranean and nourish our bodies and souls one delicious meal at a time.

Breakfast Recipes

GREEK YOGURT WITH MIXED BERRIES AND HONEY

INGREDIENTS

- 2 cups Greek yogurt (470 ml)
- 1 cup mixed berries (strawberries, blueberries, raspberries)
- 2 tablespoons honey
- A pinch of cinnamon (optional)

 Prep Time: 5 Min
Cook Time: 0 Min

 Servings: 2

DIRECTIONS

1. Divide the Greek yogurt evenly between two bowls.
2. Rinse the mixed berries and scatter them over the yogurt.
3. Drizzle each bowl with one tbsp of honey. Sprinkle ground cinnamon on top if desired.
4. Serve immediately and enjoy.

NUTRITIONAL VALUES (PER SERVING)

Calories: 250, Protein: 20g, Fat: 7g, Carbohydrates: 35g, Sugar: 30g, Fiber: 2g

MEDITERRANEAN FRITTATA WITH SPINACH AND FETA

INGREDIENTS

- 6 large eggs
- 1/2 cup milk (120 ml)
- 1 cup fresh spinach, roughly chopped
- 1/2 cup feta cheese, crumbled
- 1 small onion, finely chopped
- 2 tablespoons olive oil
- Salt and pepper to taste
- 1/4 teaspoon nutmeg (optional)

 Prep Time: 10 Min
Cook Time: 20 Min

 Servings: 4

DIRECTIONS

1. Preheat oven to 375°F (190°C). If not, you'll finish cooking the frittata on the stove.
2. Whisk the eggs, milk, salt, pepper, and nutmeg in the shallow bowl until well combined.
3. Heat two tbsp oil in a 10-inch oven-safe skillet over medium heat. Sauté the onion for 3-5 minutes.
4. Add chopped spinach to cook for 2 minutes.
5. Pour the egg mixture over the sautéed onions and spinach. Sprinkle feta cheese evenly on top.
6. Cook the frittata on the stove over medium-low heat for 5 minutes. Then, transfer the skillet to bake.
7. Bake for 13-15 minutes or until the frittata is fully set and golden. If your skillet is not oven-safe, cover and continue cooking on low heat until set.
8. Slice and serve the frittata warm.

NUTRITIONAL VALUES (PER SERVING)
Calories: 220, Protein: 14g, Fat: 16g, Carbohydrates: 4g, Sugar: 3g, Fiber: 0.5g

AVOCADO TOAST WITH OLIVE OIL AND TOMATO

INGREDIENTS

- 2 slices of whole-grain bread
- 1 ripe avocado
- 1 small tomato, sliced
- 1 tablespoon olive oil
- Salt and pepper to taste
- Red pepper flakes (optional)

Prep Time: 5 Min
Cook Time: 0 Min

Servings: 2

DIRECTIONS

1. Toast the bread slices to your preferred level of crispiness.
2. Halve the avocado and remove the pit. Scoop out the flesh and mash it.
3. Spread the mashed avocado evenly over the toasted bread slices.
4. Arrange the tomato slices on top of the avocado.
5. Drizzle olive oil over each toast. If desired, pour it with salt, crushed pepper, and red pepper flakes.
6. Serve immediately, enjoying the creamy avocado with the fresh crunch of tomato.

NUTRITIONAL VALUES (PER SERVING)

Calories: 300, Protein: 7g, Fat: 20g, Carbohydrates: 27g, Fiber: 10g, Sugar: 5g

TURKISH MENEMEN (SCRAMBLED EGGS WITH TOMATOES AND PEPPERS)

INGREDIENTS

- 6 large eggs
- 2 tablespoons olive oil
- 1 large onion, finely diced
- 1 green bell pepper, diced
- 2 tomatoes, grated or finely chopped
- Salt and pepper to taste
- 1 teaspoon paprika (optional)
- Fresh parsley, chopped for garnish

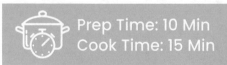 Prep Time: 10 Min
Cook Time: 15 Min

 Servings: 4

DIRECTIONS

1. Beat the eggs lightly in the deep-bottom bowl and set aside.
2. Heat two tbsp oil in a skillet over medium heat. Add diced onion and green pepper, cooking until they are softened, about 5 minutes.
3. Add the grated tomatoes, salt, pepper, and paprika. Cook more for 5 minutes until the mixture thickens slightly.
4. Reduce the heat to low and pour the beaten eggs over the tomato and pepper mixture. Let the eggs set for a minute before gently stirring to combine everything.
5. Cook until the eggs are softly set, stirring occasionally. Adjust seasoning as needed.
6. Garnish and serve warm with slices of crusty bread.

NUTRITIONAL VALUES (PER SERVING)

Calories: 220, Protein: 12g, Fat: 16g, Carbohydrates: 8g, Fiber: 2g, Sugar: 5g

FIG AND ALMOND OVERNIGHT OATS

INGREDIENTS

- 1 cup rolled oats
- 1 cup almond milk (235 ml)
- 6 dried figs, chopped
- 2 tablespoons almond butter
- 1 tablespoon chia seeds
- 1/2 teaspoon vanilla extract
- Almonds, sliced for garnish
- A pinch of salt

 Prep Time: 10 Min
Cook Time: 0 Min

 Servings: 2

DIRECTIONS

1. Combine the rolled oats, almond milk, chopped figs, almond butter, chia seeds, vanilla extract, and a pinch of salt in a mixing bowl. Stir well to combine.
2. Divide the mixture between two jars or containers with lids. Seal and refrigerate overnight or for at least 6 hours.
3. Before serving, stir the oats well. Add more almond milk if necessary.
4. Garnish with sliced almonds and additional chopped figs if desired.
5. Enjoy cold or at room temperature as a nutritious and filling breakfast.

NUTRITIONAL VALUES (PER SERVING)

Calories: 350, Protein: 10g, Fat: 14g, Carbohydrates: 50g, Fiber: 8g, Sugar: 20g

BARLEY PORRIDGE WITH DATES AND NUTS

INGREDIENTS

- 1 cup pearl barley, rinsed
- 3 cups water or milk (for a creamier texture) (710 ml)
- 1/2 cup dates, pitted and chopped
- 1/4 cup mixed nuts (almonds, walnuts, pecans), roughly chopped
- 1/2 teaspoon cinnamon
- A pinch of salt
- Optional toppings: a dollop of Greek yogurt, a drizzle of honey, fresh berries

 Prep Time: 5 Min
Cook Time: 25 Min

 Servings: 2

DIRECTIONS

1. In a medium saucepan, add water or milk to a boil. Add barley and a pinch of salt, then reduce the heat to a simmer.
2. Cook the barley, stirring occasionally, until it's tender and the liquid is mostly absorbed, about 20-25 minutes.
3. Stir in the chopped dates, mixed nuts, and cinnamon during the last 5 minutes of cooking.
4. Once cooked, divide the porridge between two bowls. Add toppings like Greek yogurt, a drizzle of honey, or fresh berries if desired.
5. Serve warm for a hearty and nutritious start to your day.

NUTRITIONAL VALUES (PER SERVING)
Calories: 330, Protein: 8g, Fat: 7g, Carbohydrates: 64g, Fiber: 12g, Sugar: 15g

SPINACH AND MUSHROOM BREAKFAST CASSEROLE

INGREDIENTS

- 8 large eggs
- 1/2 cup milk (120 ml)
- 2 cups fresh spinach, roughly chopped
- 1 cup mushrooms, sliced
- 1 small onion, diced
- 1 cup grated cheddar cheese
- 1 tablespoon olive oil
- Salt and pepper to taste

Prep Time: 15 Min
Cook Time: 35 Min

Servings: 6

DIRECTIONS

1. Preheat oven to 350°F (175°C). Grease a 9x13-inch baking dish.
2. Heat one tbsp oil in a skillet over medium heat. Sauté onion and mushrooms until softened. Add spinach and cook until wilted. Remove from heat.
3. In a large bowl, whisk together eggs and milk. Season with salt and pepper.
4. Stir in the sautéed vegetables and half of the cheese into the egg mixture.
5. Ladle the mixture into the oil-greased baking dish. Sprinkle the remaining cheese on top.
6. Bake for 35 minutes until the eggs are set, and the top is golden brown.
7. Let cool for a few minutes before slicing. Serve warmly.

NUTRITIONAL VALUES (PER SERVING)

Calories: 220, Protein: 15g, Fat: 15g, Carbohydrates: 5g, Fiber: 1g, Sugar: 3g

MEDITERRANEAN BREAKFAST QUINOA BOWL

INGREDIENTS

- 1 cup quinoa, rinsed
- 2 cups water (470 ml)
- 1/2 cup cherry tomatoes, halved
- 1/2 cucumber, diced
- 1/4 cup kalamata olives, sliced
- 1/4 cup feta cheese, crumbled
- 2 tablespoons olive oil
- Juice of 1 lemon
- Salt and pepper to taste
- 1/4 cup fresh parsley, chopped

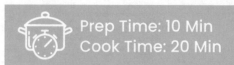 Prep Time: 10 Min
Cook Time: 20 Min

 Servings: 2

DIRECTIONS

1. In a saucepan, add water to a boil. Add quinoa, reduce heat, put the lid to cover, and simmer for 15 minutes or until water is absorbed.
2. Remove from heat, keep it covered, and put it aside for 5 minutes. Fluff with a fork.
3. Mix the cooked quinoa with tomatoes, cucumber, olives, feta cheese, olive oil, and lemon juice in a bowl. Season with salt and pepper.
4. Divide the quinoa mixture between two bowls. Garnish with chopped parsley.
5. Serve immediately, enjoying a fresh and nutritious start to your day.

NUTRITIONAL VALUES (PER SERVING)

Calories: 380, Protein: 12g, Fat: 20g, Carbohydrates: 42g, Fiber: 6g, Sugar: 4g

EGG MUFFINS WITH MEDITERRANEAN VEGETABLES

INGREDIENTS

- 10 large eggs
- 1/2 cup milk (120 ml)
- 1 cup spinach, finely chopped
- 1/2 cup bell peppers, diced
- 1/4 cup onions, diced
- 1/2 cup feta cheese, crumbled
- 1/2 cup cherry tomatoes, quartered
- Salt and pepper to taste
- 1 tablespoon olive oil (for sautéing)

 Prep Time: 10 Min
Cook Time: 20 Min

 Servings: 12

DIRECTIONS

1. Preheat oven to 375°F (190°C). Grease a 12-cup muffin pan.
2. Heat one tbsp oil in a skillet over medium heat. Sauté onions and bell peppers until softened. Add spinach and cook until wilted. Set aside to cool.
3. In a large bowl, whisk together eggs and milk. Season with salt and pepper.
4. Add the sautéed vegetables, feta cheese, and tomatoes to the egg mixture.
5. Ladle egg mixture into the muffin cups, and pour evenlyy.
6. Bake for 20 minutes or until the muffins are set and lightly golden on top.
7. Let the muffins cool in the pan for a few minutes before removing.
8. Serve warm for a quick, healthy breakfast.

NUTRITIONAL VALUES (PER SERVING)
Calories: 110, Protein: 8g, Fat: 7g, Carbohydrates: 3g, Fiber: 0.5g, Sugar: 2g

SPANISH OMELET (TORTILLA ESPAÑOLA)

INGREDIENTS

- 6 large eggs
- 1 lb (450g) potatoes, thinly sliced
- 1 large onion, thinly sliced
- 3/4 cup olive oil (180 ml)
- Salt and pepper to taste

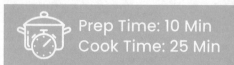

Prep Time: 10 Min
Cook Time: 25 Min

Servings: 4

DIRECTIONS

1. Heat oil over moderate heat. Add sliced potatoes and onion, seasoning with salt. Cook until the potatoes are tender but not browned, about 15 minutes.
2. In a large bowl, beat the eggs with a pinch of salt. Drain the potatoes and onions to remove the oil and add them to the eggs, mixing gently to combine.
3. Remove most of the oil from the pan (leave about 2 tablespoons) and return it to medium heat. Add the egg mixture, spreading the potatoes evenly. Cook until the bottom is golden and set, about 5 minutes.
4. Carefully shift the omelet onto a plate, then slide it back into the pan to cook the other side for about 3-4 minutes.
5. Slide the omelet to serve, either hot or cold, and cut into wedges.

NUTRITIONAL VALUES (PER SERVING)
Calories: 450, Protein: 14g, Fat: 35g, Carbohydrates: 23g, Fiber: 3g, Sugar: 2g

RICOTTA AND HONEY ON WHOLE GRAIN BREAD

INGREDIENTS

- 2 slices whole grain bread
- 1/2 cup ricotta cheese
- 2 tablespoons honey
- 1/4 teaspoon cinnamon (optional)
- Fresh berries for topping (optional)

 Prep Time: 5 Min
Cook Time: 0 Min

 Servings: 2

DIRECTIONS

1. Toast the whole grain bread to your preference.
2. Spread the ricotta cheese evenly over each slice of toasted bread.
3. Drizzle honey over the ricotta, and sprinkle with cinnamon if using.
4. Top with fresh berries and serve immediately.

NUTRITIONAL VALUES (PER SERVING)

Calories: 270, Protein: 14g, Fat: 9g, Carbohydrates: 35g, Fiber: 4g, Sugar: 16g

Salad and Side Recipes

MEDITERRANEAN TUNA SALAD

INGREDIENTS

- 2 cans (each 5 oz) tuna in olive oil, drained
- 1/2 cup diced red bell pepper
- 1/2 cup diced cucumber
- 1/4 cup finely chopped red onion
- 1/4 cup chopped Kalamata olives
- 2 tablespoons capers, rinsed
- Juice of 1 lemon
- 3 tablespoons extra virgin olive oil
- Salt and pepper to taste
- Fresh basil leaves for garnish

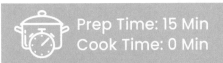 Prep Time: 15 Min
Cook Time: 0 Min

 Servings: 4

DIRECTIONS

1. Combine the tuna, red bell pepper, cucumber, red onion, olives, and capers in a large, deep-bottom bowl.
2. In a small shallow bowl, toss the lemon juice and olive oil. Pour over the tuna mixture. Powder it with salt and pepper to taste. Gently toss to combine all the ingredients.
3. Garnish with fresh basil leaves before serving. Serve over a bed of greens or with whole-grain bread.

NUTRITIONAL VALUES (PER SERVING)

Calories: 250, Protein: 20g, Fat: 15g, Carbohydrates: 6g, Fiber: 1g, Sugar: 3g

TABBOULEH WITH SHRIMP

INGREDIENTS

- 1 cup bulgur wheat
- 1 1/2 cups boiling water (350 ml)
- 1 lb shrimp, peeled and deveined
- 2 tablespoons olive oil
- Juice of 2 lemons
- 1 cup parsley, finely chopped
- 1/2 cup mint leaves, finely chopped
- 2 tomatoes, diced
- 1 cucumber, diced
- Salt and pepper to taste

Prep Time: 20 Min
Cook Time: 5 Min

Servings: 4

DIRECTIONS

1. Place the bulgur in a large, deep-bottom bowl. Pour boiling water over it, keep it covered, and let it stand for 20 minutes until absorbed. Fluff with a fork.
2. In a pan, heat one tbsp oil over medium-high heat. Add shrimp and cook for 2-3 minutes for each side side. Set aside to cool, then chopped.
3. Add the lemon juice, leftover oil, parsley, mint, tomatoes, and cucumber to the bulgur. Powder it with salt and pepper. Mix well.
4. Gently fold in the cooked shrimp. Serve chilled or at room temperature.

NUTRITIONAL VALUES (PER SERVING)

Calories: 320, Protein: 25g, Fat: 10g, Carbohydrates: 35g, Fiber: 8g, Sugar: 5g

CHICKPEA AND CHORIZO SALAD

INGREDIENTS

- 1 can (15 oz weight) chickpeas, drained and rinsed
- 6 ounces chorizo, diced
- 2 tablespoons olive oil
- 1 red bell pepper, diced
- 1 small red onion, thinly sliced
- 2 cloves garlic, minced
- Juice of 1 lemon
- 1/4 cup chopped fresh parsley
- Salt and pepper to taste

 Prep Time: 15 Min
Cook Time: 10 Min

 Servings: 4

DIRECTIONS

1. Heat one tbsp oil in a skillet over medium heat. Add chorizo and cook for 5 minutes. Remove the chorizo and set aside.
2. Add the leftover oil, red bell pepper, red onion, and garlic. Sauté until softened, about 5 minutes.
3. Combine the chickpeas, cooked chorizo, sautéed vegetables, lemon juice, and parsley in a large deep-bottom bowl. Toss until well mixed. Powder it with salt and crushed pepper to taste.
4. Serve as it is chilled, adjusting seasoning as needed.

NUTRITIONAL VALUES (PER SERVING)

Calories: 350, Protein: 18g, Fat: 20g, Carbohydrates: 27g, Fiber: 6g, Sugar: 5g

BEETROOT AND GOAT CHEESE SALAD

INGREDIENTS

- 4 medium beetroots, cooked and sliced
- 1 cup goat cheese, crumbled
- 1/4 cup walnuts, toasted and chopped
- 2 tablespoons balsamic vinegar
- 4 tablespoons olive oil
- Salt and pepper to taste
- Mixed salad greens

 Prep Time: 15 Min
Cook Time: 0 Min

 Servings: 4

DIRECTIONS

1. Arrange the mixed salad greens in a salad bowl. Top with sliced beetroots, crumbled goat cheese, and toasted walnuts.
2. Toss the balsamic vinegar and olive oil in a small shallow bowl. Powder it with salt and pepper.
3. Drizzle dressing just before serving.
4. Toss gently to combine and serve immediately.

NUTRITIONAL VALUES (PER SERVING)

Calories: 300, Protein: 10g, Fat: 24g, Carbohydrates: 12g, Fiber: 3g, Sugar: 8g

GRILLED PEACH AND BURRATA SALAD WITH BALSAMIC GLAZE

INGREDIENTS

- 4 ripe peaches, halved and pitted
- 1 tablespoon olive oil
- 8 ounces burrata cheese
- 2 cups arugula
- 1/4 cup balsamic glaze
- Salt and freshly ground black pepper
- Fresh basil leaves for garnish

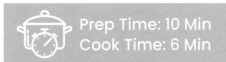 Prep Time: 10 Min
Cook Time: 6 Min

 Servings: 4

DIRECTIONS

1. Preheat the grill to medium-high heat. Brush peach halves with olive oil.
2. Grill peaches cut-side down for about 3-4 minutes, then flip and grill for another 2-3 minutes until tender and grill marks appear.
3. Arrange arugula on a serving platter. Place grilled peaches on top.
4. Tear the burrata and scatter over the peaches and arugula.
5. Drizzle with balsamic glaze and Powder it with salt and pepper.
6. Garnish and serve immediately.

NUTRITIONAL VALUES (PER SERVING)
Calories: 290, Protein: 14g, Fat: 20g, Carbohydrates: 18g, Fiber: 2g, Sugar: 16g

ARUGULA, FIG, AND PROSCIUTTO SALAD

INGREDIENTS

- 6 cups fresh arugula leaves
- 6 fresh figs, quartered
- 6 slices of prosciutto, torn into bite-sized pieces
- ½ cup crumbled feta cheese
- ¼ cup chopped walnuts
- 2 tablespoons extra virgin olive oil
- 2 tablespoons balsamic vinegar
- Salt and pepper to taste

Prep Time: 15 Min
Cook Time: 0 Min

Servings: 4

DIRECTIONS

1. In a large mixing bowl, combine the fresh arugula leaves, quartered figs, torn prosciutto pieces, crumbled feta cheese, and chopped walnuts.
2. In a small bowl, whisk together the extra virgin olive oil and balsamic vinegar to make the dressing.
3. Pour the dressing over the salad ingredients and toss gently to coat everything evenly.
4. Season the salad with salt and pepper to taste.
5. Serve immediately as a delicious and refreshing appetizer or light main course.

NUTRITIONAL VALUES (PER SERVING)
Calories: 235, Protein: 9g, Fat: 15g, Carbohydrates: 18g, Fiber: 4g, Sugar: 12g

LENTIL SALAD WITH SAUSAGE AND FETA

INGREDIENTS

- 1 cup dried lentils
- 4 Italian sausages, sliced
- 1 red bell pepper, diced
- 1 small red onion, finely chopped
- 2 cloves garlic, minced
- 2 tablespoons olive oil
- 2 tablespoons red wine vinegar
- 1 teaspoon dried oregano
- Salt and pepper to taste
- ½ cup crumbled feta cheese
- Fresh parsley for garnish (optional)

 Prep Time: 15 Min
Cook Time: 25 Min

 Servings: 4

DIRECTIONS

1. Rinse the lentils under cold water and drain them. Place them in a medium saucepan and cover with water. Bring to a boil, then reduce the heat to low and simmer for about 20-25 minutes, or until the lentils are tender but still firm. Drain any excess water and set aside to cool.
2. While the lentils are cooking, heat 1 tablespoon of olive oil in a skillet over medium heat. Add the sliced Italian sausages and cook until browned and cooked through, about 8-10 minutes. Remove from the skillet and set aside.
3. In the same skillet, add the remaining olive oil and sauté the diced red bell pepper, chopped red onion, and minced garlic until softened, about 5 minutes.
4. In a large mixing bowl, combine the cooked lentils, cooked sausage slices, sautéed vegetables, red wine vinegar, dried oregano, salt, and pepper. Toss everything together until well combined.
5. Gently fold in the crumbled feta cheese.
6. Taste and adjust seasoning if needed. Garnish with fresh parsley if desired.
7. Serve the lentil salad warm or at room temperature as a hearty and flavorful Mediterranean dish.

NUTRITIONAL VALUES (PER SERVING)

Calories: 460, Protein: 23g, Fat: 25g, Carbohydrates: 34g, Fiber: 10g, Sugar: 4g

GARLIC ROASTED ASPARAGUS WITH LEMON ZEST

INGREDIENTS

- 1 lb asparagus, ends trimmed
- 3 tablespoons olive oil
- 3 cloves garlic, minced
- Zest of 1 lemon
- Salt and crushed pepper to taste

 Prep Time: 5 Min
Cook Time: 15 Min

 Servings: 4

DIRECTIONS

1. Preheat oven to 400°F (200°C). Place the asparagus on the baking sheet in one layer.
2. Drizzle oil and sprinkle with mashed garlic, lemon zest, salt, and pepper. Toss to evenly coat.
3. Roast for 13-15 minutes until asparagus is tender and lightly browned.
4. Serve immediately with garnish.

NUTRITIONAL VALUES (PER SERVING)

Calories: 110, Protein: 3g, Fat: 9g, Carbohydrates: 6g, Fiber: 3g, Sugar: 2g

BALSAMIC GLAZED BRUSSELS SPROUTS

INGREDIENTS

- 1 lb Brussels sprouts, trimmed and halved
- 2 tablespoons olive oil
- Salt and crushed pepper, to taste
- 3 tablespoons balsamic vinegar
- 2 teaspoons honey (optional for a sweeter glaze)

 Prep Time: 10 Min
Cook Time: 20 Min

 Servings: 4

DIRECTIONS

1. Preheat oven to 425°F (220°C). Toss the Brussels sprouts with two tbsp oil, salt, and crushed pepper. Spread them out in a single layer.
2. Roast for 20 minutes or until tender and caramelized, stirring halfway through. In the last few minutes of roasting, drizzle the balsamic vinegar (and honey) over the Brussels sprouts and toss to coat.
3. Roast for another 2-3 minutes to glaze. Adjust seasoning if necessary. Serve hot, garnished with additional balsamic glaze if desired.

NUTRITIONAL VALUES (PER SERVING)

Calories: 250, Protein: 20g, Fat: 7g, Carb: 35g, Sugar: 30g, Fiber: 2g

CRISPY PARMESAN POLENTA FRIES

INGREDIENTS

- 18 oz (about 500g) pre-cooked polenta, cut into fries
- 2 tablespoons olive oil
- 1/2 cup grated Parmesan cheese
- Salt and pepper to taste
- Marinara sauce for dipping (optional)

Prep Time: 5 Min
Cook Time: 25 Min

Servings: 4

DIRECTIONS

1. Preheat oven to 425°F (220°C). Arrange the baking sheet with parchment paper. Toss the polenta fries with olive oil, salt, and pepper In the deep-bottom bowl.
2. Arrange them on the paper-arranged baking sheet in a single layer. Bake for 15 minutes, flip the fries, and sprinkle with grated Parmesan cheese.
3. Continue baking for 8-10 minutes or until crispy and golden. Serve hot with marinara sauce for dipping if desired.

NUTRITIONAL VALUES (PER SERVING)
Calories: 220, Protein: 6g, Fat: 10g, Carbohydrates: 28g, Fiber: 2g, Sugar: 1g

Fish and Seafood Recipes

GRILLED SEA BREAM WITH LEMON AND HERBS

INGREDIENTS

- 4 sea bream fillets
- 2 tablespoons olive oil
- Juice and zest of 1 lemon
- 2 cloves garlic, minced
- 1 tablespoon fresh rosemary, chopped
- 1 tablespoon fresh thyme, chopped
- Salt and pepper to taste
- Lemon wedges and fresh herbs for garnish

Prep Time: 10 Min
Cook Time: 10 Min

Servings: 4

DIRECTIONS

1. Mix olive oil, lemon juice and zest, garlic, rosemary, thyme, salt, and crushed pepper in a small, deep-bottom bowl.
2. Place the sea bream fillets in a dish and pour the marinade over them. Ensure each fillet is well-coated. Cover and refrigerate for thirty minutes.
3. Preheat the grill to medium-high heat. Oil the grill grates to prevent sticking. Remove the fillets from the marinade and grill each side for 4-5 minutes. Serve immediately with garnish ingredients.

NUTRITIONAL VALUES (PER SERVING)

Calories: 200, Protein: 24g, Fat: 11g, Carbohydrates: 1g, Fiber: 0g, Sugar: 0g

SEAFOOD PAELLA

INGREDIENTS

- 2 tablespoons olive oil
- 1 onion, finely chopped
- 2 cloves garlic, minced
- 1 red bell pepper, chopped
- 1 cup Arborio rice
- 1/2 teaspoon saffron threads
- 2 1/2 cups chicken or seafood broth
- 1 cup canned diced tomatoes
- 1 lb mixed seafood (shrimp, mussels, clams, and squid rings)
- 1/2 cup frozen peas
- Salt and pepper to taste
- Lemon wedges for serving
- Fresh parsley, chopped for garnish

Prep Time: 15 Min
Cook Time: 35 Min

Servings: 4

DIRECTIONS

1. Heat two tbsp oil over medium heat in a large skillet or paella pan. Add onion, garlic, and bell pepper. Cook until softened.
2. Stir in Arborio rice and saffron, coating the rice well with the oil and vegetables.
3. Add broth and diced tomatoes; bring them to a simmer, then reduce the heat to low. Cook, uncovered, for about 20 minutes.
4. Gently stir in the mixed seafood and peas. Cover and cook for 10-15 minutes until seafood is cooked through and rice is tender.
5. Powder it with salt and pepper. Serve hot with garnish elements.

NUTRITIONAL VALUES (PER SERVING)

Calories: 400, Protein: 30g, Fat: 10g, Carbohydrates: 50g, Fiber: 3g, Sugar: 5g

BAKED COD WITH OLIVES AND LEMON

INGREDIENTS

- 4 cod fillets (about 6 oz each)
- 2 tablespoons olive oil
- Salt and pepper to taste
- 1 lemon, thinly sliced
- 1/2 cup halved Kalamata olives, pitted
- 2 cloves garlic, minced
- 1 tablespoon capers, rinsed
- Fresh parsley, chopped for garnish

Prep Time: 10 Min
Cook Time: 20 Min

Servings: 4

DIRECTIONS

1. Preheat oven to 400°F (200°C). Arrange the baking sheet with parchment paper.
2. Place the cod fillets on the paper-arranged baking sheet. Drizzle with olive oil and Powder it with salt and pepper.
3. Top each fillet with lemon slices, olives, minced garlic, and capers.
4. Bake for 18-20 minutes until the cod is opaque and flakes easily with a fork.
5. Serve immediately, garnished with fresh parsley.

NUTRITIONAL VALUES (PER SERVING)

Calories: 220, Protein: 23g, Fat: 12g, Carbohydrates: 4g, Fiber: 1g, Sugar: 0g

SHRIMP SAGANAKI WITH FETA AND TOMATOES

INGREDIENTS

- 1 lb large shrimp, peeled and deveined
- 2 tablespoons olive oil
- 1 onion, diced
- 2 cloves garlic, minced
- 1 can (14 oz) diced tomatoes
- 1/2 cup feta cheese, crumbled
- 1/4 cup fresh parsley, chopped
- Salt and pepper to taste
- 1/4 teaspoon red pepper flakes (optional)

 Prep Time: 10 Min
Cook Time: 15 Min

 Servings: 4

DIRECTIONS

1. Heat two tbsp oil in a large skillet over medium heat. Add diced onion and mashed garlic, and sauté until softened.
2. Add diced tomatoes (with liquid) and bring to a simmer. Powder it with salt, pepper, and red pepper flakes if used.
3. Add shrimp, stirring to coat them with the tomato mixture. Cook for 4-5 minutes.
4. Sprinkle crumbled feta over the shrimp. Cover and cook for 2-3 minutes, until the feta is slightly melted.
5. Garnish with fresh parsley before serving.

NUTRITIONAL VALUES (PER SERVING)
Calories: 260, Protein: 25g, Fat: 14g, Carbohydrates: 8g, Fiber: 2g, Sugar: 4g

SICILIAN SWORDFISH ROLLS (INVOLTINI DI PESCE SPADA)

INGREDIENTS

- 8 thin swordfish steaks (about 2 oz each)
- 1/2 cup breadcrumbs
- 1/4 cup grated Parmesan cheese
- 2 tablespoons olive oil
- 2 cloves garlic, minced
- 1/4 cup pine nuts
- 1/4 cup raisins
- 1/4 cup fresh parsley, chopped
- Salt and pepper to taste
- Lemon wedges for serving

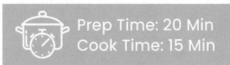

Prep Time: 20 Min
Cook Time: 15 Min

Servings: 4

DIRECTIONS

1. In the deep-bottom bowl, combine breadcrumbs, Parmesan cheese, 2 tablespoons olive oil, garlic, pine nuts, raisins, and parsley. Powder it with salt and pepper.
2. Lay out the swordfish steaks and spread the breadcrumb mixture among them evenly.
3. Roll up each steak and secure it with a toothpick.
4. Put the large skillet with olive oil over medium-high heat. Cook the swordfish rolls for 2-3 minutes per side or until golden and cooked through.
5. Serve immediately with lemon wedges.

NUTRITIONAL VALUES (PER SERVING)
Calories: 320, Protein: 27g, Fat: 18g, Carbohydrates: 12g, Fiber: 1g, Sugar: 5g

OCTOPUS SALAD WITH OLIVE OIL AND LEMON

INGREDIENTS

- 1 lb cooked octopus, cut into bite-sized pieces
- 1/4 cup extra virgin olive oil (60 ml)
- Juice of 1 lemon
- 2 cloves garlic, minced
- 1/4 cup fresh parsley, chopped
- Salt and crushed black pepper to taste
- Lemon wedges for serving

Prep Time: 15 Min
Cook Time: 1 Hr 30 Min

Servings: 4

DIRECTIONS

1. Instructions:
2. If the octopus is not pre-cooked, boil it in a pot of salted water with a cork (a traditional method believed to tenderize the meat) for about 1.5 hours or until tender. Let cool, then cut into pieces.
3. In a large, deep-bottom bowl, combine the cooked octopus, olive oil, lemon juice, minced garlic, and chopped parsley. Season with salt and pepper to taste.
4. Toss well to ensure the octopus is evenly coated with the dressing.
5. Chill for one hour before serving
6. with lemon wedges.

NUTRITIONAL VALUES (PER SERVING)

Calories: 200, Protein: 25g, Fat: 10g, Carbohydrates: 5g, Fiber: 0g, Sugar: 0g

GRILLED SARDINES WITH GARLIC AND PARSLEY

INGREDIENTS

- 16 fresh sardines, cleaned and gutted
- 2 tablespoons olive oil
- 4 cloves garlic, minced
- 1/4 cup fresh parsley, chopped
- Salt and crushed black pepper to taste
- Lemon wedges for serving

 Prep Time: 10 Min
Cook Time: 10 Min

 Servings: 4

DIRECTIONS

1. Preheat your grill to medium-high heat.
2. Rinse the sardines under cold water and pat dry with paper towels.
3. Mix the olive oil, minced garlic, and chopped parsley in a small, deep-bottom bowl. Powder it with salt and pepper.
4. Brush the sardines with the garlic and parsley oil on both sides.
5. Grill the sardines on each side for 2-3 minutes until the skin is crispy and the flesh is cooked through.
6. Serve immediately with lemon wedges.

NUTRITIONAL VALUES (PER SERVING)

Calories: 220, Protein: 25g, Fat: 12g, Carbohydrates: 2g, Fiber: 0g, Sugar: 0g

SALMON CARPACCIO WITH CAPERS AND DILL

INGREDIENTS

- 1 lb fresh salmon fillet, skin removed
- 2 tablespoons extra virgin olive oil
- Juice of 1 lemon
- 2 tablespoons capers, rinsed
- 2 tablespoons fresh dill, chopped
- Salt and crushed black pepper to taste
- Lemon wedges for serving

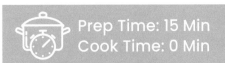

Prep Time: 15 Min
Cook Time: 0 Min

Servings: 4

DIRECTIONS

1. Place the salmon fillet in the freezer for about 15 minutes to firm up, making it easier to slice thinly.
2. Use the sharp knife, slice the salmon as thinly as possible, and place them on the serving platter.
3. Drizzle the olive oil and lemon juice evenly over the salmon slices.
4. Sprinkle the capers and dill over the salmon. Powder it with salt and pepper to taste.
5. Chill for 10 minutes before serving to allow the flavors to meld.
6. Serve with lemon wedges on the side.

NUTRITIONAL VALUES (PER SERVING)
Calories: 240, Protein: 23g, Fat: 15g, Carbohydrates: 1g, Fiber: 0g, Sugar: 0g

TUNA STEAKS WITH CAPER AND OLIVE SAUCE

INGREDIENTS

- 4 tuna steaks (about 6 oz each)
- 2 tablespoons olive oil
- Salt and crushed black pepper to taste
- For the Sauce:
- 1/4 cup olives, pitted and chopped
- 2 tablespoons capers, rinsed
- 2 cloves garlic, minced
- Juice of 1 lemon
- 2 tablespoons parsley, chopped
- 3 tablespoons olive oil

 Prep Time: 10 Min
Cook Time: 10 Min

 Servings: 4

DIRECTIONS

1. Preheat the grill to high heat. Brush the tuna steaks with oil and powder it with salt and pepper.
2. Grill the tuna for 2-3 minutes on each side for medium-rare or longer to your desired level of doneness.
3. Mix the olives, capers, garlic, lemon juice, parsley, and oil in a deep-bottom bowl for the sauce.
4. Once the tuna is grilled, place each steak on a plate and spoon the caper and olive sauce.
5. Serve immediately.

NUTRITIONAL VALUES (PER SERVING)

Calories: 330, Protein: 40g, Fat: 18g, Carbohydrates: 2g, Fiber: 0g, Sugar: 0g

GRILLED LOBSTER WITH GARLIC-PARSLEY BUTTER

INGREDIENTS

- 2 whole lobsters, split in half
- 4 tablespoons butter, melted
- 2 cloves garlic, minced
- 2 tablespoons fresh parsley, chopped
- Salt and pepper to taste
- Lemon wedges for serving

Prep Time: 15 Min
Cook Time: 10 Min

Servings: 4

DIRECTIONS

1. Preheat your grill to medium-high heat.
2. Mix the melted butter, garlic, parsley, salt, and pepper in a small, deep-bottom bowl.
3. Brush the garlic-parsley butter over the cut sides of the lobster halves.
4. Place the lobsters on the grill, shell side down, and grill for 5-7 minutes until the meat is opaque and cooked. Serve immediately with lemon wedges.

NUTRITIONAL VALUES (PER SERVING)
Calories: 240, Protein: 22g, Fat: 16g, Carbohydrates: 2g, Fiber: 0g, Sugar: 0g

CATALAN FISH STEW (SUQUET DE PEIX)

INGREDIENTS

- 2 tablespoons olive oil
- 1 onion, finely chopped
- 3 cloves garlic, minced
- 1 red bell pepper, chopped
- 2 tomatoes, peeled and chopped
- 1 lb mixed fish fillets (such as cod, snapper), cut into chunks
- 8 oz clams, scrubbed
- 8 oz shrimp, peeled and deveined
- 4 cups fish stock
- 1/2 teaspoon saffron threads
- 1/4 cup white wine
- Salt and pepper to taste
- Fresh parsley, chopped for garnish

Prep Time: 25 Min
Cook Time: 40 Min

Servings: 4

DIRECTIONS

1. In a large pot, heat two tbsp of oil over medium heat. Add diced onion, mashed garlic, and bell pepper. Sauté until softened.
2. Add tomatoes and cook for 5-6 minutes.
3. Add the fish chunks, clams, shrimp, fish stock, saffron, salt, pepper, and white wine.
4. Bring to a simmer for about 30 minutes or until the seafood is cooked and the clams have opened. Discard any unopened clams.
5. Garnish with fresh parsley before serving.

NUTRITIONAL VALUES (PER SERVING)

Calories: 320, Protein: 36g, Fat: 10g, Carbohydrates: 15g, Fiber: 2g, Sugar: 5g

Pizza, Wrap, and Sandwich Recipes

SPICY CHORIZO AND SERRANO HAM PIZZA

INGREDIENTS

- Pizza Dough Ingredients:
- 2 1/4 teaspoons (1 packet) active dry yeast
- 1 cup warm water (about 110°F or 45°C)
- 2 1/2 cups all-purpose flour
- 1 teaspoon sugar
- 1 teaspoon salt
- 2 tablespoons olive oil
- Toppings Ingredients:
- 1/2 cup tomato sauce
- 1 cup mozzarella cheese, shredded
- 1/2 cup chorizo, thinly sliced
- 1/2 cup Serrano ham, thinly sliced
- 1 teaspoon red pepper flakes
- Fresh basil leaves for garnish

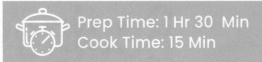 Prep Time: 1 Hr 30 Min
Cook Time: 15 Min

 Servings: 4

DIRECTIONS

1. Prepare the Pizza Dough:
2. In a small shallow bowl, dissolve yeast and sugar in warm water. Let stand until bubbly, about 7-10 minutes.
3. In a large, deep-bottom bowl, combine flour and salt. Add yeast mixture and olive oil. Stir until the dough forms.
4. Turn the dough on the flour-dusted surface and knead for 8 minutes.
5. Place the dough in a bowl, covering it with a damp cloth. Let it rise for 1 hour.
6. Assemble and Bake the Pizza:
7. Preheat oven to 475°F (245°C).
8. Punch down the dough and turn it out on the flour-dusted surface. Roll or stretch it into your desired shape.
9. Spread tomato sauce, leaving a small border around the edges.
10. Sprinkle shredded mozzarella cheese over the sauce. Arrange the chorizo and Serrano ham slices on top. Sprinkle with red pepper flakes.
11. Transfer the pizza, and bake for 12-15 minutes. Garnish with fresh basil leaves before serving.

NUTRITIONAL VALUES (PER SERVING)
Calories: 620, Protein: 28g, Fat: 26g, Carbohydrates: 72g, Fiber: 3g, Sugar: 4g

MUSHROOM AND GOAT CHEESE PIZZA

INGREDIENTS

- Pizza Dough Ingredients:
- 2 1/4 teaspoons (1 packet) active dry yeast
- 1 cup warm water
- 2.5 cups all-purpose flour
- 1 teaspoon sugar
- 1 teaspoon salt
- 2 tablespoons olive oil
- Toppings Ingredients:
- 2 tablespoons olive oil, divided
- 2 cups sliced mushrooms (cremini or button)
- Salt and pepper to taste
- 1/2 cup goat cheese, crumbled
- 1 cup arugula
- 1/4 cup shaved Parmesan cheese
- Balsamic glaze for drizzling (optional)

 Prep Time: 1 Hr 30 Min
Cook Time: 15 Min

 Servings: 4

DIRECTIONS

1. In a small shallow bowl, dissolve yeast and sugar in warm water. Let stand until frothy, about 5 to 10 minutes.
2. In the deep-bottom bowl, combine flour and salt. Add the yeast mixture and olive oil. Stir until the dough forms.
3. Turn the dough on the flour-dusted surface and knead for 8 minutes.
4. Place the dough in a bowl, covering it with a damp cloth. Let it rise for one hour.
5. Preheat oven to 475°F (245°C).
6. Heat one tbsp oil in a skillet over medium heat. Add mushrooms, Powder them with salt and pepper, and sauté until golden brown. Set aside.
7. Punch down the dough and turn it out on the flour-dusted surface. Roll or stretch it into your desired shape.
8. Transfer the dough to the parchment paper. Brush with remaining olive oil.
9. Evenly distribute the sautéed mushrooms and crumbled goat cheese over the dough.
10. Transfer the pizza (with parchment) to the preheated pizza stone or baking sheet. Bake for 12-15 minutes.
11. Top the hot pizza with fresh arugula and shaved Parmesan. Drizzle with balsamic glaze if desired.
12. Slice and serve immediately.

NUTRITIONAL VALUES (PER SERVING)

Calories: 630, Protein: 22g, Fat: 27g, Carbohydrates: 76g, Fiber: 4g, Sugar: 5g

SHRIMP AND PESTO PIZZA

INGREDIENTS

- Pizza Dough Ingredients:
- Follow the same recipe as above.
- Toppings Ingredients:
- 2 tablespoons pesto sauce
- 1/2 lb shrimp, peeled and deveined
- 1/2 cup sun-dried tomatoes, chopped
- 1 cup mozzarella cheese, shredded
- 1/2 cup arugula
- 2 tablespoons olive oil
- Salt and pepper to taste

 Prep Time: 1 Hr 30 Min
Cook Time: 15 Min

 Servings: 4

DIRECTIONS

1. In a small shallow bowl, dissolve yeast and sugar in warm water. Let stand until frothy, about 5 to 10 minutes.
2. In the deep-bottom bowl, combine flour and salt. Add the yeast mixture and olive oil. Stir until the dough forms.
3. Turn the dough on the flour-dusted surface and knead for 8 minutes.
4. Place the dough in the bowl, covering it with a damp cloth. Let it rise for 1 hour.
5. Prep the Shrimp:
6. In a skillet, heat one tbsp oil over medium heat. Season the shrimp with salt and pepper. Sauté until pink and cook through, about 2-3 minutes per side. Remove from heat.
7. Assemble and Bake the Pizza:
8. Preheat oven to 475°F (245°C). Roll out the dough on a floured surface to your desired thickness. Transfer it to the parchment paper piece.
9. Spread pesto over the dough, leaving a small border around the edges.
10. Scatter the cooked shrimp and sun-dried tomatoes over the pesto. Top with shredded mozzarella.
11. Slide the pizza (with parchment) onto the preheated stone or a baking sheet. Bake for 12-15 minutes. Remove from oven and spread arugula on top. Drizzle with the leftover olive oil. Slice and serve immediately.

NUTRITIONAL VALUES (PER SERVING)

Calories: 650, Protein: 32g, Fat: 28g, Carbohydrates: 74g, Fiber: 4g, Sugar: 5g

SPINACH AND RICOTTA PIZZA

INGREDIENTS

- Pizza Dough Ingredients:
- Follow the same dough recipe as above.
- Toppings Ingredients:
- 2 tablespoons olive oil
- 2 cloves garlic, minced
- 2 cups fresh spinach leaves
- 1 cup ricotta cheese
- 1 cup cherry tomatoes, halved
- Salt and pepper to taste

Prep Time: 1 Hr 30 Min
Cook Time: 15 Min

Servings: 4

DIRECTIONS

1. Prepare the Pizza Dough:
2. Follow the dough instructions as provided in the previous recipe.
3. Assemble and Bake the Pizza:
4. Preheat oven to 475°F (245°C). Roll out the dough on a floured surface. Transfer to a baking sheet or preheated pizza stone.
5. Brush the dough with oil and sprinkle minced garlic evenly. Distribute spinach leaves over the dough, dollop with ricotta cheese, and scatter cherry tomatoes on top.
6. Powder it with salt and pepper. Bake for 12-15 minutes.
7. Serve immediately, optionally drizzled with a bit more olive oil.

NUTRITIONAL VALUES (PER SERVING)

Calories: 540, Protein: 18g, Fat: 20g, Carbohydrates: 72g, Fiber: 4g, Sugar: 5g

GREEK CHICKEN GYRO WRAP

INGREDIENTS

- For the Chicken:
- 1 lb. chicken breast, thinly sliced
- 2 tablespoons olive oil
- Juice of 1 lemon
- 2 cloves garlic, minced
- 1 teaspoon dried oregano
- Salt and pepper to taste
- For the Tzatziki:
- 1 cup Greek yogurt
- 1/2 cucumber, grated and drained
- 1 clove garlic, minced
- 1 tablespoon olive oil
- 1 tablespoon lemon juice
- Salt to taste
- Fresh dill, chopped (optional)
- Additional Ingredients:
- 4 large flatbreads or pita bread
- 1 tomato, sliced
- 1/2 red onion, thinly sliced

 Prep Time: 20 Min
Cook Time: 20 Min

 Servings: 4

DIRECTIONS

1. Marinate the Chicken:
2. In the deep-bottom bowl, pour the oil, lemon juice, garlic, oregano, salt, and pepper. Add chicken slices and marinate for at least 1 hour in the refrigerator.
3. Prepare the Tzatziki:
4. Mix Greek yogurt, grated cucumber, garlic, olive oil, lemon juice, salt, and dill in a deep-bottom bowl. Refrigerate until needed.
5. Cook the Chicken:
6. Heat a grill pan over medium-high heat. Cook the chicken until golden and cooked, about 5-7 minutes per side.
7. Assemble the Gyros:
8. Warm the flatbreads. Spread a generous amount of tzatziki on each flatbread, add cooked chicken, tomato slices, and red onion, and roll up the flatbread to form a wrap. Serve immediately.

NUTRITIONAL VALUES (PER SERVING)
Calories: 540, Protein: 38g, Fat: 22g, Carbohydrates: 48g, Fiber: 3g, Sugar: 5g

FALAFEL WRAP WITH HUMMUS

INGREDIENTS

- 8 falafel balls (homemade or store-bought)
- 4 large flatbreads or pita bread
- 1/2 cup hummus
- 1 cup tabbouleh salad
- For the Tahini Sauce:
- 1/4 cup tahini
- 2 tablespoons lemon juice
- 1 clove garlic, minced
- Water, as needed, to thin
- Salt to taste

Prep Time: 30 Min
Cook Time: 10 Min

Servings: 4

DIRECTIONS

1. Prepare the Tahini Sauce:
2. Whisk together tahini, lemon juice, garlic, and a pinch of salt in a deep-bottom bowl. Gradually add water to get the right consistency.
3. Assemble the Wraps:
4. Warm the flatbreads. Spread hummus on each flatbread, add two falafel balls (crushed or whole), and top with tabbouleh.
5. Drizzle tahini sauce and roll up the flatbread to form a wrap. Serve immediately.

NUTRITIONAL VALUES (PER SERVING)

Calories: 500, Protein: 18g, Fat: 20g, Carbohydrates: 64g, Fiber: 10g, Sugar: 8g

LAMB KOFTA WRAP

INGREDIENTS

- For the Lamb Kofta:
- 1 lb ground lamb
- 2 cloves garlic, minced
- 1 small onion, finely chopped
- 2 tablespoons fresh mint, chopped
- 1 teaspoon ground cumin
- Salt and pepper to taste
- For the Yogurt Sauce:
- 1 cup Greek yogurt
- 1/2 cucumber, grated and drained
- 2 tablespoons fresh mint, chopped
- 1 clove garlic, minced
- Salt to taste
- Additional Ingredients:
- 4 large flatbreads or pita bread
- 1 tomato, sliced
- 1/2 red onion, thinly sliced

 Prep Time: 30 Min
Cook Time: 10 Min

 Servings: 4

DIRECTIONS

1. Prepare the Lamb Kofta:
2. Mix ground lamb, mashed garlic, onion, mint, cumin, salt, and pepper in a deep-bottom bowl. Form into small sausages or patties. Set aside.
3. Prepare the Yogurt Sauce:
4. Toss the Greek yogurt, grated cucumber, chopped mint, mashed garlic, and salt in a small shallow bowl. Mix well and chill before using.
5. Cook the Lamb Kofta:
6. Preheat a grill pan to medium-high heat. Cook the lamb kofta for 4-5 minutes for each side.
7. Assemble the Wraps:
8. Warm the flatbread or pita bread. Spread the yogurt sauce layer on each flatbread, place a couple of lamb kofta in the center, and top with tomato slices and red onion.
9. Roll up the flatbread tightly to enclose the filling.
10. Serve the lamb kofta wraps immediately, accompanied by any leftover yogurt sauce for dipping.

NUTRITIONAL VALUES (PER SERVING)

Calories: 620, Protein: 35g, Fat: 32g, Carbohydrates: 48g, Fiber: 3g, Sugar: 5g

MUFFULETTA WITH OLIVE SALAD, CURED MEATS, AND CHEESE

INGREDIENTS

- For the Olive Salad:
- 1 cup mixed olives, pitted and chopped
- 1/4 cup pickled cauliflower, chopped
- 2 tablespoons capers, rinsed
- 1/4 cup roasted red peppers, chopped
- 1 garlic clove, minced
- 1/4 cup extra virgin olive oil
- 2 tablespoons red wine vinegar
- 1 teaspoon dried oregano
- Salt and pepper to taste
- For the Sandwich:
- 1 large round loaf Italian bread, sliced in half horizontally
- ¼ lb. salami, thinly sliced
- ¼ lb. ham, thinly sliced
- ¼ lb. mortadella, thinly sliced
- ¼ lb. provolone cheese, sliced
- ¼ lb. mozzarella cheese, sliced

 Prep Time: 20 Min
Cook Time: 0 Min

 Servings: 4

DIRECTIONS

1. Prepare the Olive Salad:
2. Combine olives, cauliflower, capers, roasted red peppers, garlic, olive oil, vinegar, oregano, salt, and pepper in a deep-bottom bowl. Mix well and refrigerate for one hour or overnight for flavors to meld.
3. Assemble the Muffuletta:
4. Scoop out some of the bread from the bottom half of the loaf to make room for the fillings.
5. Spread a generous olive salad over the bottom half, including some of the oil.
6. Layer the salami, ham, mortadella, provolone, and mozzarella on the olive salad.
7. Place the top half of the bread on top and press down gently.
8. Wrap the sandwich tightly in plastic wrap and let it sit for at least an hour, or refrigerate overnight to allow the flavors to soak into the bread. Cut into wedges and serve.

NUTRITIONAL VALUES (PER SERVING)

Calories: 650, Protein: 35g, Fat: 45g, Carbohydrates: 35g, Fiber: 4g, Sugar: 5g

GRILLED HALLOUMI SANDWICH

INGREDIENTS

- 8 slices halloumi cheese
- 8 slices of hearty bread
- 2 tomatoes, sliced
- 1 cup arugula
- 2 tablespoons olive oil
- Balsamic glaze for drizzling
- Salt and pepper to taste

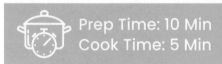

Prep Time: 10 Min
Cook Time: 5 Min

Servings: 4

DIRECTIONS

1. Put the grill pan over moderate heat and brush with olive oil. Grill the halloumi slices for 2-3 minutes for each side, or until they have nice grill marks and are slightly softened.
2. Toast the bread slices for one minute for each side or until lightly toasted.
3. Assemble the sandwiches by placing a grilled halloumi layer on four bread slices.
4. Top with tomato slices, Powder it with salt and pepper, and add a handful of arugula.
5. Drizzle with balsamic glaze, then top with the remaining bread slices.
6. Serve immediately.

NUTRITIONAL VALUES (PER SERVING)

Calories: 420, Protein: 22g, Fat: 25g, Carbohydrates: 30g, Fiber: 3g, Sugar: 5g

MEDITERRANEAN TUNA SALAD SANDWICH

INGREDIENTS

- 2 cans (5 ounces each) of tuna in olive oil, drained
- 1/4 cup chopped Kalamata olives, pitted
- 2 tablespoons capers, rinsed
- 1/4 cup red onion, finely chopped
- 2 tablespoons fresh parsley, chopped
- Juice of 1 lemon
- 2 tablespoons olive oil
- Salt and crushed black pepper to taste
- 8 slices of whole-grain or sourdough bread
- Lettuce leaves

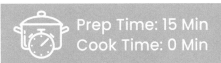 Prep Time: 15 Min
Cook Time: 0 Min

 Servings: 4

DIRECTIONS

1. Mix the tuna, olives, capers, red onion, parsley, lemon juice, and olive oil in the deep-bottom bowl. Season with salt and pepper to taste.
2. Arrange lettuce leaves on 4 slices of bread. Divide the tuna salad evenly among the slices.
3. Top with the remaining bread slices. Press gently.
4. Serve immediately, cut into halves or quarters as preferred.

NUTRITIONAL VALUES (PER SERVING)

Calories: 330, Protein: 25g, Fat: 15g, Carbohydrates: 26g, Fiber: 4g, Sugar: 5g

SARDINE AND TOMATO SANDWICH

INGREDIENTS

- 2 cans (4 ounces each) of sardines in olive oil, drained
- 1 tomato, sliced
- 1 cup shredded cabbage
- Juice of 1 lemon
- 2 tablespoons mayonnaise (optional)
- 8 slices of rye or whole-grain bread
- Salt and crushed black pepper to taste

 Prep Time: 10 Min
Cook Time: 0 Min

 Servings: 4

DIRECTIONS

1. In a small, deep-bottom bowl, gently break apart the sardines with a fork. Mix with lemon juice and mayonnaise (if using). Powder it with salt and pepper.
2. Arrange the shredded cabbage on 4 slices of bread. Top with tomato slices.
3. Divide the sardine mixture evenly among the sandwiches.
4. Top with the remaining bread slices. Press gently.
5. Serve immediately, enjoying the zesty and hearty flavors.

NUTRITIONAL VALUES (PER SERVING)
Calories: 290, Protein: 20g, Fat: 14g, Carbohydrates: 24g, Fiber: 5g, Sugar: 4g

Poultry and Turkey Recipes

CHICKEN SOUVLAKI WITH TZATZIKI SAUCE

INGREDIENTS

- For the Chicken Souvlaki:
- 1 lb chicken breast, cut into cubes
- 2 tablespoons olive oil
- Juice of 1 lemon
- 2 cloves garlic, minced
- 1 teaspoon dried oregano
- Salt and pepper to taste
- For the Tzatziki Sauce:
- 1 cup Greek yogurt
- 1/2 cucumber, grated and drained
- 1 clove garlic, minced
- 1 tablespoon olive oil
- 1 tablespoon lemon juice
- Salt to taste
- Fresh dill, chopped (optional)
- Additional:
- Pita bread for serving
- Chopped tomatoes and onions for serving

 Prep Time: 25 Min
Cook Time: 10 Min

 Servings: 4

DIRECTIONS

1. Mix olive oil, lemon juice, garlic, oregano, salt, and pepper in the shallow bowl. Add chicken cubes and marinate in the refrigerator for one hour, preferably overnight.
2. For the tzatziki, combine Greek yogurt, grated cucumber, garlic, one tbsp oil, lemon juice, salt, and dill in a shallow bowl. Refrigerate until serving.
3. Preheat a grill to its medium-high heat. Thread the chicken cubes onto skewers. Grill for 10 minutes, turning occasionally.
4. Warm the pita bread on the grill. Serve the chicken souvlaki with pita bread, tzatziki sauce, and chopped tomatoes and onions.

NUTRITIONAL VALUES (PER SERVING)

Calories: 320, Protein: 28g, Fat: 16g, Carbohydrates: 12g, Fiber: 1g, Sugar: 3g

MOROCCAN CHICKEN TAGINE WITH APRICOTS AND ALMONDS

INGREDIENTS

- 1 lb chicken thighs, bone-in and skin-on
- 2 tablespoons olive oil
- 1 onion, chopped
- 2 cloves garlic, minced
- 1 teaspoon ground cumin
- 1 teaspoon ground cinnamon
- 1/2 teaspoon ground ginger
- 1/2 teaspoon ground turmeric
- 1 cup chicken broth
- 1/2 cup dried apricots, chopped
- 1/4 cup almonds, toasted
- Salt and pepper to taste
- Fresh cilantro for garnish

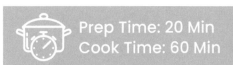

Prep Time: 20 Min
Cook Time: 60 Min

Servings: 4

DIRECTIONS

1. Heat two tbsp oil in a tagine or large pot over medium heat. Powder the chicken with salt and crushed pepper. Add to the large pot and sear on both sides. Remove and set aside.
2. Add diced onion and mashed garlic. Cook until softened. Stir in cumin, cinnamon, ginger, and turmeric until fragrant.
3. Return the chicken to the pot. Add chicken broth and take to a simmer. Cover and cook for about 45 minutes.
4. Add the apricots to the pot. Continue to cook uncovered for 15 minutes.
5. Garnish with toasted almonds and fresh cilantro. Serve hot with couscous or bread.

NUTRITIONAL VALUES (PER SERVING)

Calories: 420, Protein: 25g, Fat: 24g, Carbohydrates: 28g, Fiber: 4g, Sugar: 16g

ITALIAN CHICKEN CACCIATORE

INGREDIENTS

- 1 lb chicken thighs, bone-in and skin-on
- 2 tablespoons olive oil
- 1 onion, sliced
- 1 bell pepper, sliced
- 2 cloves garlic, minced
- 1 can (28 oz) diced tomatoes
- 1/2 cup red wine (optional)
- 1 teaspoon dried oregano
- 1 teaspoon dried basil
- Salt and pepper to taste
- Fresh parsley, for garnish

Prep Time: 15 Min
Cook Time: 45 Min

Servings: 4

DIRECTIONS

1. In a large skillet, Heat two tbsp oil over medium-high heat. Powder chicken with salt and pepper, and brown on both sides. Remove from the skillet and
2. put them aside.
3. Add diced onion, bell pepper, and garlic. Cook until softened.
4. Add diced tomatoes, red wine (if used), oregano, and basil. Return the chicken to the skillet. Bring to a simmer.
5. Cover and cook on low heat for about 35 minutes until the chicken is cooked through.
6. Garnish with fresh parsley before serving.

NUTRITIONAL VALUES (PER SERVING)
Calories: 350, Protein: 25g, Fat: 20g, Carbohydrates: 15g, Fiber: 3g, Sugar: 8g

GREEK LEMON-OREGANO ROASTED CHICKEN

INGREDIENTS

- 4 chicken thighs, bone-in and skin-on
- 2 tablespoons olive oil
- Juice of 2 lemons
- 2 teaspoons dried oregano
- 4 cloves garlic, minced
- Salt and crushed black pepper to taste
- 1 lemon, sliced for garnish
- Fresh oregano, for garnish

Prep Time: 15 Min
Cook Time: 60 Min

Servings: 4

DIRECTIONS

1. Preheat oven to 375°F (190°C).
2. In a small, deep-bottom bowl, combine olive oil, lemon juice, dried oregano, minced garlic, salt, and pepper. Mix well.
3. Arrange the chicken thighs in a roasting pan. Pour the lemon-oregano mixture over the chicken, ensuring each piece is well coated.
4. Place lemon slices around the chicken in the pan.
5. Roast in the preheated oven for one hour.
6. Garnish with fresh oregano before serving.

NUTRITIONAL VALUES (PER SERVING)

Calories: 420, Protein: 31g, Fat: 32g, Carbohydrates: 3g, Fiber: 1g, Sugar: 1g

INGREDIENTS

- 1 lb chicken breast, cut into pieces
- 2 tablespoons olive oil
- 1 onion, finely chopped
- 2 cloves garlic, minced
- 1 cup orzo pasta
- 2 cups chicken broth
- 1 can (14 oz) diced tomatoes, undrained
- 1 teaspoon dried oregano
- 1 teaspoon dried basil
- Salt and pepper to taste
- 1/2 cup sliced Kalamata olives, pitted
- 1/2 cup crumbled feta cheese
- Fresh parsley, chopped for garnish

Prep Time: 15 Min
Cook Time: 30 Min

Servings: 4

DIRECTIONS

1. Heat one tbsp oil in a skillet over medium-high heat. Add the chicken pieces, Powder them with salt and crushed pepper, and cook until browned and cooked through. Remove the meat and set aside.
2. Add the leftover oil, onion, and garlic in the same skillet. Cook until the onion is translucent.
3. Stir the orzo and cook it until it becomes lightly toasted
4. , stirring often.
5. Add the oregano, basil, salt, pepper, diced tomatoes with juice, and chicken broth and stir. After taking it to a boil, lower the heat to a simmer. After the orzo is soft and most of the liquid has been absorbed, cook it covered for about fifteen minutes.
6. After cooking, add the Kalamata olives back to the skillet. Cook for five more minutes to ensure it's thoroughly heated.
7. Serve sprinkled with crumbled feta cheese and garnished with fresh parsley.

NUTRITIONAL VALUES (PER SERVING)

Calories: 460, Protein: 35g, Fat: 18g, Carbohydrates: 40g, Fiber: 3g, Sugar: 5g

SICILIAN CHICKEN WITH CAPERS AND OLIVES

INGREDIENTS

- 4 chicken thighs, bone-in and skin-on
- Salt and pepper to taste
- 2 tablespoons olive oil
- 1 onion, sliced
- 2 cloves garlic, minced
- 1/2 cup white wine (optional)
- 1 can (14 oz) diced tomatoes
- 1 tablespoon capers, rinsed
- 1/2 cup green olives, pitted
- 1 teaspoon dried oregano
- Fresh basil leaves for garnish

 Prep Time: 20 Min
Cook Time: 40 Min

 Servings: 4

DIRECTIONS

1. Preheat oven to 375°F (190°C).
2. Powder the chicken thighs with salt and pepper.
3. Heat two tbsp oil in the ovenproof skillet over moderate heat. Add meat, skin-side down, and cook for 5 minutes. Flip and cook for another 5 minutes. Remove chicken and set aside.
4. In the same skillet, add the onion and garlic. Cook until softened, about 5 minutes.
5. Add white wine to deglaze, then scrape up any browned bits.
6. Stir in the diced tomatoes, capers, olives, and oregano.
7. Return the chicken, nestling it into the sauce.
8. Transfer the skillet and bake uncovered for 25-30 minutes.
9. Garnish with fresh basil leaves before serving.

NUTRITIONAL VALUES (PER SERVING)

Calories: 410, Protein: 24g, Fat: 28g, Carbohydrates: 12g, Fiber: 2g, Sugar: 4g

CHICKEN MEATBALLS WITH ZUCCHINI NOODLES

INGREDIENTS

- For the Chicken Meatballs:
- 1 lb ground chicken
- 1/4 cup breadcrumbs
- 1/4 cup grated Parmesan cheese
- 1 egg, beaten
- 2 cloves garlic, minced
- 1 teaspoon Italian seasoning
- Salt and pepper to taste
- For the Zucchini Noodles:
- 4 zucchinis, spiralized into noo-dles
- 1 tablespoon olive oil
- Salt to taste
- Additional:
- Marinara sauce for serving
- Fresh basil for garnish

 Prep Time: 20 Min
Cook Time: 20 Min

 Servings: 4

DIRECTIONS

1. Preheat oven to 375°F (190°C). Arrange the baking sheet with parchment paper.
2. In a shallow bowl, toss the ground chicken with breadcrumbs, Parmesan, egg, garlic, Italian season-ing, salt, and crushed pepper. Mix well.
3. Form the mixture into one-inch meatballs and place on a paper-arranged baking sheet.
4. Bake for 15-20 minutes. While baking, heat one tbsp oil in a skillet over medium heat. Add the zuc-chini noodles and sauté for 3-4 minutes until tender. Powder it with salt.
5. Serve the meatballs over the zucchini noodles with marinara sauce and garnish with fresh basil.

NUTRITIONAL VALUES (PER SERVING)
Calories: 330, Protein: 28g, Fat: 18g, Carbohydrates: 12g, Fiber: 3g, Sugar: 6g

TURKEY KOFTAS WITH TZATZIKI

INGREDIENTS

- For the Turkey Koftas:
- 1 lb ground turkey
- 1 onion, finely grated
- 2 cloves garlic, minced
- 2 tablespoons fresh parsley, chopped
- 1 teaspoon ground cumin
- 1/2 teaspoon ground coriander
- 1/2 teaspoon paprika
- Salt and pepper to taste
- For the Tzatziki:
- 1 cup Greek yogurt
- 1/2 cucumber, grated and drained
- 1 clove garlic, minced
- 2 tablespoons olive oil
- 1 tablespoon lemon juice
- Salt to taste
- Fresh dill, chopped (optional)
- Wooden or metal skewers

Prep Time: 30 Min
Cook Time: 10 Min

Servings: 4

DIRECTIONS

1. Prepare the Koftas:
2. Combine ground turkey, grated onion, garlic, parsley, cumin, coriander, paprika, salt, and pepper in the deep-bottom bowl. Mix well.
3. Form the mixture into elongated koftas around skewers. Chill in the refrigerator for about 20 minutes to firm up.
4. Make the Tzatziki:
5. Toss the Greek yogurt with grated cucumber, garlic, two tbsp olive oil, lemon juice, salt, and dill in a deep-bottom bowl. Refrigerate until needed.
6. Cook the Koftas:
7. Preheat a grill to its moderate heat. Grill the koftas for about 8-10 minutes, turning occasionally, until cooked through.
8. Serve the turkey koftas with tzatziki on the side.

NUTRITIONAL VALUES (PER SERVING)
Calories: 320, Protein: 28g, Fat: 18g, Carbohydrates: 8g, Fiber: 1g, Sugar: 4g

MEDITERRANEAN STUFFED TURKEY BREAST

INGREDIENTS

- 1 large turkey breast, butterflied
- 1/2 cup spinach, chopped
- 1/4 cup sun-dried tomatoes, chopped
- 1/4 cup feta cheese, crumbled
- 2 cloves garlic, minced
- 2 tablespoons fresh basil, chopped
- Salt and pepper to taste
- 2 tablespoons olive oil

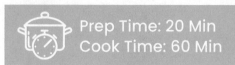
Prep Time: 20 Min
Cook Time: 60 Min

Servings: 4

DIRECTIONS

1. Preheat oven to 375°F (190°C). Lay the butterflied turkey breast flat and powder both sides with salt and pepper.
2. Spread the spinach, sun-dried tomatoes, feta cheese, garlic, and basil over one side of the turkey breast. Roll up the turkey breast tightly and secure it with kitchen twine.
3. Heat two tbsp oil in a skillet over medium-high heat. Brown the turkey roll on all sides.
4. Place the skillet and roast for about 45-60 minutes.
5. Let rest for 10 minutes before slicing. Serve slices with pan juices drizzled over the top.

NUTRITIONAL VALUES (PER SERVING)
Calories: 380, Protein: 55g, Fat: 14g, Carbohydrates: 6g, Fiber: 1g, Sugar: 3g

TURKEY MOUSSAKA

INGREDIENTS

- 1 lb ground turkey
- 2 eggplants, sliced
- 2 tablespoons olive oil
- 1 onion, chopped
- 2 cloves garlic, minced
- 1 can (14 oz) crushed tomatoes
- 1 teaspoon cinnamon
- 1/2 teaspoon allspice
- Salt and pepper to taste
- For the Béchamel Sauce:
- 2 tablespoons butter
- 2 tablespoons all-purpose flour
- 1 1/2 cups milk
- 1/4 cup grated Parmesan cheese
- Nutmeg to taste
- Salt and pepper to taste

Prep Time: 30 Min
Cook Time: 60 Min

Servings: 4

DIRECTIONS

1. Preheat oven to 350°F (175°C). Brush eggplant slices with olive oil and powder with salt. Arrange on the paper-arranged baking sheet and bake for 20 minutes, until soft.
2. In a skillet, heat one tbsp oil over medium heat. Add diced onion and mashed garlic and cook until softened. Add minced turkey, breaking it up with a spoon, and cook until browned.
3. Stir in the crushed tomatoes, cinnamon, allspice, salt, and ground pepper, and simmer for 10 minutes.
4. Prepare the Béchamel Sauce:
5. Put the saucepan over medium heat to melt the butter. Add flour and cook, stirring, for one-two minutes, or until a smooth paste forms.
6. Stir in the milk gradually, making sure there are no lumps. Cook until the sauce thickens enough, stirring constantly.
7. Take off the stove and mix in the Parmesan cheese. Powder with nutmeg, salt, and pepper.
8. Assemble the Moussaka:
9. Layer half of the baked eggplant slices in a baking dish. Top with the turkey mixture, then with the remaining eggplant slices. Pour the béchamel sauce over the top, spreading it evenly.
10. Bake for 26-30 minutes until the top is golden and bubbly.
11. Let it sit for 7-10 minutes before serving. This allows the layers to set, making it easier to cut and serve.

NUTRITIONAL VALUES (PER SERVING)

Calories: 450, Protein: 35g, Fat: 22g, Carbohydrates: 28g, Fiber: 6g, Sugar: 12g

SPICED TURKEY BURGERS WITH CUCUMBER AND YOGURT

INGREDIENTS

- For the Turkey Burgers:
- 1 lb ground turkey
- 2 cloves garlic, minced
- 1 teaspoon ground cumin
- 1/2 teaspoon smoked paprika
- 1/4 teaspoon cayenne pepper
- Salt and pepper to taste
- 4 whole wheat hamburger buns
- For the Cucumber Yogurt Sauce:
- 1 cup Greek yogurt
- 1/2 cucumber, grated and drained
- 2 tablespoons fresh mint, chopped
- 1 clove garlic, minced
- 1 tablespoon lemon juice
- Salt to taste
- Additional toppings: sliced tomatoes, lettuce

 Prep Time: 20 Min
Cook Time: 10 Min

 Servings: 4

DIRECTIONS

1. Make the Turkey Burgers:
2. Combine the ground turkey, minced garlic, cumin, smoked paprika, cayenne, salt, and pepper in the deep-bottom bowl. Mix well and form into 4 patties.
3. Prepare the Cucumber Yogurt Sauce:
4. Mix the Greek yogurt, grated cucumber, chopped mint, minced garlic, lemon juice, and salt in the other deep-bottom bowl. Refrigerate until needed.
5. Cook the Burgers:
6. Heat a grill over medium heat. Grill the turkey burgers for 4-5 minutes for each side or until fully cooked.
7. Assemble the Burgers:
8. Serve the turkey burgers on whole wheat buns with cucumber yogurt sauce, sliced tomatoes, and lettuce.

NUTRITIONAL VALUES (PER SERVING)

Calories: 370, Protein: 28g, Fat: 18g, Carbohydrates: 24g, Fiber: 3g, Sugar: 6g

Beef, Lamb, and Pork Recipes

ITALIAN BEEF BRACIOLE

INGREDIENTS

- 4 thin slices of beef round or flank steak
- Salt and pepper to taste
- 4 cloves garlic, minced
- 1/2 cup grated Parmesan cheese
- 1/4 cup fresh parsley, chopped
- 2 tablespoons olive oil
- 1 cup dry white wine
- 1 can (28 oz) crushed tomatoes
- 1 onion, finely chopped
- 1 teaspoon dried oregano
- 1/2 teaspoon red pepper flakes

 Prep Time: 30 Min
Cook Time: 2 Hour

 Servings: 4

DIRECTIONS

1. Lay out the beef slices on a work surface. Powder it with salt and pepper. Sprinkle each slice with garlic, Parmesan, and parsley. Roll up the slices tightly and secure them with toothpicks or kitchen twine.
2. Heat two tbsp oil in a skillet over medium-high heat. Brown the meat rolls on all sides, then remove from the skillet.
3. Add onion and cook until softened. Add the white wine to scrape up any browned bits from the bottom. Reduce the wine by half.
4. Add the crushed tomatoes, oregano, and red pepper flakes. Powder it with salt and pepper. Return the beef rolls to the skillet and spoon the sauce over them.
5. Cover and simmer on low flame for about 2 hours or until the beef is tender. Turn the rolls occasionally and add water if the sauce gets too thick.
6. Serve the beef braciole with the tomato sauce, removing the toothpicks or twine before serving.

NUTRITIONAL VALUES (PER SERVING)
Calories: 450, Protein: 35g, Fat: 25g, Carbohydrates: 12g, Fiber: 2g, Sugar: 5g

SPANISH BEEF EMPANADAS

INGREDIENTS

- 1 lb ground beef
- 2 tablespoons olive oil
- 1 onion, chopped
- 2 cloves garlic, minced
- 1/2 cup green olives, chopped
- 1/2 cup raisins
- 2 teaspoons paprika
- Salt and pepper to taste
- 1 package refrigerated pie crusts (2 crusts)
- 1 egg, beaten for egg wash

Prep Time: 45 Min
Cook Time: 20 Min

Servings: 4

DIRECTIONS

1. Heat two tbsp in a skillet over medium heat. Add diced onion and mashed garlic and cook until softened. Add minced beef and cook until browned.
2. Stir in the olives, raisins, paprika, salt, and pepper. Cook for another 5 minutes. Let the filling cool.
3. Preheat oven to 400°F (200°C). Roll out the pie and cut out rounds using a large cookie cutter or cup.
4. Place a spoonful of the beef mixture in the center of each round. Spread the dough over the filling and press the edges to seal. Use a fork to crimp the edges. Brush the tops with egg wash.
5. Bake for 17-20 minutes until the empanadas are golden brown.
6. Serve hot.

NUTRITIONAL VALUES (PER SERVING)

Calories: 580, Protein: 25g, Fat: 35g, Carbohydrates: 42g, Fiber: 3g, Sugar: 10g

BISTECCA FIORENTINA

INGREDIENTS

- 1 T-bone steak (about 2 inches thick)
- Salt and crushed black pepper to taste
- 2 tablespoons olive oil
- 4 cloves garlic, lightly crushed
- A few sprigs of fresh rosemary

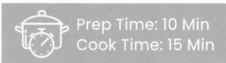

Prep Time: 10 Min
Cook Time: 15 Min

Servings: 4

DIRECTIONS

1. Let the steak come to room temperature for about 30 minutes before grilling. Then, sprinkle it with salt and crushed pepper.
2. Preheat a grill or grill pan. Rub the steak with olive oil, garlic, and rosemary.
3. Depending on the thickness, grill the steak for 5-7 minutes per side for medium-rare. Use the rosemary sprigs to baste the steak with more olive oil while it cooks.
4. Let it rest for 10 minutes, then slice. Serve with additional olive oil and fresh rosemary.

NUTRITIONAL VALUES (PER SERVING)
Calories: 750, Protein: 65g, Fat: 55g, Carbohydrates: 0g, Fiber: 0g, Sugar: 0g

GREEK BEEF STIFADO

INGREDIENTS

- 2 lbs beef stew meat, cubed
- 1/4 cup olive oil
- 10 small onions, peeled and left whole
- 4 cloves garlic, minced
- 1 can (14 oz) diced tomatoes
- 1/2 cup red wine
- 2 tablespoons red wine vinegar
- 1 teaspoon ground cinnamon
- 1 bay leaf
- Salt and pepper to taste
- Fresh parsley for garnish

Prep Time: 20 Min
Cook Time: 2 Hour

Servings: 4

DIRECTIONS

1. Heat one-fourth cup of oil in a pot over medium-high heat. Brown the meat cubes on all sides and set aside.
2. Add the whole onions in the same pot and cook until they soften. Add garlic and cook for another minute.
3. Return the beef to the pot. Add diced tomatoes, red wine, vinegar, cinnamon, bay leaf, salt, and pepper.
4. Bring to a boil, then decrease the stove heat. Cover and simmer for 2 hours.
5. Remove the bay leaf before serving, and take with garnish elements and rice or potatoes.

NUTRITIONAL VALUES (PER SERVING)
Calories: 580, Protein: 52g, Fat: 26g, Carbohydrates: 34g, Fiber: 4g, Sugar: 14g

ITALIAN SAUSAGE AND PEPPERS

INGREDIENTS

- 1 lb Italian sausages (mild or spicy)
- 2 tablespoons olive oil
- 2 bell peppers, sliced
- 1 large onion, sliced
- 2 cloves garlic, minced
- 1 teaspoon dried oregano
- Salt and pepper to taste
- Fresh basil for garnish

Prep Time: 15 Min
Cook Time: 25 Min

Servings: 4

DIRECTIONS

1. Over medium-high heat, sear the sausages until browned on all sides, about 10 minutes. Remove from the skillet and slice.
2. Add olive oil, bell peppers, diced onion, and mashed garlic to the skillet. Powder it with oregano, salt, and pepper. Cook over medium flame until the vegetables are softened and slightly caramelized, about 15 minutes.
3. Return the sliced sausages to the skillet with the vegetables and heat through.
4. Garnish with fresh basil before serving.

NUTRITIONAL VALUES (PER SERVING)

Calories: 480, Protein: 22g, Fat: 38g, Carbohydrates: 12g, Fiber: 2g, Sugar: 6g

CATALAN PORK RIBS WITH HONEY

INGREDIENTS

- 2 lbs pork ribs
- Salt and crusehd black pepper to taste
- 2 tablespoons olive oil
- 4 cloves garlic, minced
- 1/2 cup white wine
- 1/2 cup chicken broth
- 1/4 cup honey
- 1 tablespoon apple cider vinegar
- 1 teaspoon smoked paprika
- 1 teaspoon dried thyme
- Fresh parsley, chopped for garnish

Prep Time: 15 Min
Cook Time: 1 hr 30 Min

Servings: 4

DIRECTIONS

1. Preheat oven to 325°F (165°C). Powder the pork ribs with salt and pepper.
2. Heat two tbsp oil over medium-high heat in a large ovenproof skillet or roasting pan. Add the ribs and brown on all sides. Transfer the ribs to a plate.
3. Add mashed garlic and sauté until fragrant in the same skillet, about 1 minute. Deglaze the pan with white wine to scrape up any browned bits.
4. Stir in the chicken broth, honey, apple cider vinegar, smoked paprika, and thyme. Bring to a simmer.
5. Return the ribs to the skillet and coat them with the sauce. Cover with foil and place to roast.
6. Roast for 1 hour 30 minutes, basting occasionally with the sauce, until the ribs are tender.
7. Remove the ribs and let them rest for a few minutes. Garnish with fresh parsley before serving.

NUTRITIONAL VALUES (PER SERVING)

Calories: 600, Protein: 35g, Fat: 45g, Carbohydrates: 20g, Fiber: 0g, Sugar: 18g

PORK SCALOPPINI WITH LEMON AND CAPERS

INGREDIENTS

- 1 lb pork tenderloin, sliced into ½-inch thick medallions
- Salt and crushed black pepper to taste
- 1/4 cup all-purpose flour
- 2 tablespoons olive oil
- 1/4 cup lemon juice
- 1/2 cup chicken broth
- 2 tablespoons capers, rinsed
- 2 tablespoons unsalted butter
- Fresh parsley, chopped for garnish
- Lemon slices, for garnish

 Prep Time: 15 Min
Cook Time: 10 Min

 Servings: 4

DIRECTIONS

1. Powder the pork medallions with salt and pepper, then dredge in flour and jerk to remove the excess.
2. In a skillet, heat two tbsp oil over medium-high heat. Add pork and cook on both sides, 2-3 minutes per side. Transfer to a plate.
3. Ladle chicken broth with lemon juice into the same skillet. Scoop up any browned bits from the pan's bottom and bring to a boil.
4. Once the butter has melted and the sauce has somewhat thickened, turn down the heat and stir in the capers and butter.
5. Put the pork back in the skillet and cover it with sauce. Cook for another 1-2 minutes.
6. Serve the pork scaloppini garnished with fresh parsley and lemon slices.

NUTRITIONAL VALUES (PER SERVING)

Calories: 320, Protein: 24g, Fat: 20g, Carbohydrates: 10g, Fiber: 0g, Sugar: 0g

RACK OF LAMB WITH HERB CRUST

INGREDIENTS

- 1 rack of lamb (about 8 ribs), trimmed
- Salt and crushed black pepper to taste
- 2 tablespoons olive oil
- 2 cloves garlic, minced
- 1 cup breadcrumbs
- 2 tablespoons fresh rosemary, chopped
- 2 tablespoons fresh thyme, chopped
- 1/4 cup Dijon mustard
- 1/4 cup grated Parmesan cheese

 Prep Time: 20 Min
Cook Time: 25 Min

 Servings: 4

DIRECTIONS

1. Preheat oven to 400°F (200°C).
2. Powder the rack of lamb with salt and pepper. Heat two tbsp oil in a skillet over high heat. Add meat rack and sear until browned on all sides, for 3-4 minutes. Remove from heat.
3. Mix breadcrumbs, rosemary, thyme, and Parmesan cheese in a bowl.
4. Brush the rack with Dijon mustard, then press the breadcrumb mixture onto the mustard-coated lamb.
5. Place the meat rack on the roasting rack in a roasting pan. Roast for 20-25 minutes for medium-rare or until the crust is golden and the lamb reaches your desired doneness.
6. Let it rest for 10 minutes before slicing between the ribs and serving.

NUTRITIONAL VALUES (PER SERVING)

Calories: 450, Protein: 24g, Fat: 30g, Carbohydrates: 20g, Fiber: 2g, Sugar: 2g

MOROCCAN LAMB TAGINE WITH APRICOTS

INGREDIENTS

- 2 lbs lamb shoulder, cut into 2-inch pieces
- 2 tablespoons olive oil
- 1 large onion, chopped
- 2 cloves garlic, minced
- 1 teaspoon ground cinnamon
- 1 teaspoon ground cumin
- 1/2 teaspoon ground ginger
- 2 cups water or lamb broth
- 1 cup dried apricots, halved
- 1/2 cup almonds, toasted
- Salt and pepper to taste
- Fresh cilantro for garnish

Prep Time: 20 Min
Cook Time: 2 Hour

Servings: 4

DIRECTIONS

1. Heat olive oil in a tagine or large pot over medium-high heat. Powder the lamb with salt and pepper, and brown in batches. Remove the lamb and set aside.
2. Add diced onion and mashed garlic, cooking until softened. Stir in cinnamon, cumin, and ginger.
3. Return the lamb to the pot. Add water or broth and bring to a simmer. Cover and cook on low heat for about 1.5 hours or until tender.
4. Add apricots to the tagine and cook for an additional 30 minutes.
5. Garnish with toasted almonds and fresh cilantro before serving with couscous or bread.

NUTRITIONAL VALUES (PER SERVING)

Calories: 600, Protein: 38g, Fat: 36g, Carbohydrates: 38g, Fiber: 6g, Sugar: 28g

GREEK LAMB GYRO

INGREDIENTS

- 1 lb lamb leg or shoulder, thinly sliced
- 2 tablespoons olive oil
- Juice of 1 lemon
- 2 cloves garlic, minced
- 1 teaspoon dried oregano
- Salt and pepper to taste
- 4 pita breads
- For the Tzatziki:
- 1 cup Greek yogurt
- 1/2 cucumber, grated and drained
- 1 clove garlic, minced
- 2 tablespoons olive oil
- 1 tablespoon lemon juice
- Salt to taste
- Additional toppings: sliced tomatoes, sliced onions

Prep Time: 25 Min
Cook Time: 10 Min

Servings: 4

DIRECTIONS

1. Marinate the lamb with olive oil, lemon juice, garlic, oregano, salt, and pepper. Refrigerate for two hours or overnight.
2. Preheat a grill over medium-high heat. Cook the lamb slices until browned and cooked, about 3-4 minutes per side.
3. Prepare the tzatziki by mixing Greek yogurt, grated cucumber, mashed garlic, olive oil, lemon juice, and salt.
4. Warm the pita breads. Place cooked lamb on each pita, add tzatziki sauce, and top with sliced tomatoes and onions.
5. Roll up the pita around the fillings and serve immediately.

NUTRITIONAL VALUES (PER SERVING)

Calories: 510, Protein: 32g Fat: 24g, Carbohydrates: 42g, Fiber: 3g, Sugar: 6g

ITALIAN LAMB OSSO BUCO

INGREDIENTS

- 4 lamb shanks
- Salt and pepper to taste
- 1/4 cup all-purpose flour
- 3 tablespoons olive oil
- 1 onion, chopped
- 1 carrot, chopped
- 1 stalk celery, chopped
- 4 cloves garlic, minced
- 1 cup dry white wine
- 2 cups beef or lamb broth
- 1 can (14 oz) diced tomatoes
- 1 teaspoon fresh thyme leaves
- 2 bay leaves
- Fresh parsley, chopped for garnish

Prep Time: 20 Min
Cook Time: 2 Hour

Servings: 4

DIRECTIONS

1. Powder lamb shanks with salt and pepper, then dredge in flour.
2. Brown the Lamb:
3. Heat two tbsp oil in a Dutch oven or heavy pot over medium-high heat. Add shank meat and brown on all sides. Remove and set aside.
4. Sauté the Vegetables:
5. Add chopped onion, carrot, celery, and mashed garlic to the same pot. Cook until softened.
6. Pour white wine to deglaze the pot, scraping up any browned bits. Add broth, diced tomatoes, thyme, and bay leaves. Return lamb shanks to the pot. Bring to a simmer, then put the lid and transfer to a 325°F (165°C) oven. Braise for about 2 hours or until the lamb is tender.
7. Remove bay leaves. Garnish the lamb osso buco with fresh parsley before serving, ideally with risotto or mashed potatoes.

NUTRITIONAL VALUES (PER SERVING)
Calories: 650, Protein: 48g, Fat: 32g, Carbohydrates: 24g, Fiber: 4g, Sugar: 6g

Snacks and Appetizer Recipes

HUMMUS CLASSIC WITH OLIVE OIL DRIZZLE

INGREDIENTS

- 1 can (15 oz weight) chickpeas, drained and rinsed
- 1/4 cup tahini
- 2 tablespoons olive oil
- Juice of 1 lemon
- 2 cloves garlic, minced
- Salt to taste
- 1/2 teaspoon ground cumin
- Water, as needed for consistency
- Paprika, for garnish
- Fresh parsley, chopped for garnish

 Prep Time: 10 Min
Cook Time: 0 Min

 Servings: 4

DIRECTIONS

1. Combine chickpeas, tahini, olive oil, lemon juice, garlic, salt, and cumin in a food blender. Blend until smooth.
2. If the hummus looks thick, add water, one tbsp at a time.
3. Transfer the hummus to a serving bowl. Create a small well in the center and drizzle with additional olive oil.
4. Sprinkle paprika powder and chopped parsley over the top for garnish.
5. Serve with pita bread, vegetables, or your favorite dipping snacks.

NUTRITIONAL VALUES (PER SERVING)

Calories: 220, Protein: 7g, Fat: 14g, Carbohydrates: 18g, Fiber: 5g, Sugar: 3g

SPANAKOPITA TRIANGLES (SPINACH AND FETA PHYLLO)

INGREDIENTS

- 1/2 lb fresh spinach, chopped
- 1 cup feta cheese, crumbled
- 1/4 cup fresh dill, chopped
- 1/4 cup green onions, chopped
- 2 eggs, lightly beaten
- Salt and pepper to taste
- 1/2 cup unsalted butter, melted
- 12 sheets of phyllo dough, thawed

Prep Time: 30 Min
Cook Time: 20 Min

Servings: 4

DIRECTIONS

1. Preheat oven to 375°F (190°C). Arrange the baking sheet with parchment paper.
2. Combine spinach, feta cheese, dill, green onions, and eggs in a large mixing bowl. Powder it with salt and pepper.
3. Lay one phyllo dough sheet on a clean surface and lightly brush with melted butter. Place another sheet on top of the previous one and brush with butter again. Cut the stacked sheets into 4 strips.
4. Place a spoonful of the spinach mixture at one end of each strip. Fold the excess phyllo dough over the filling to form a triangle, continuing to fold in a triangle pattern until the strip is fully wrapped around the filling.
5. Place the triangles on the parchment paper-arranged baking sheet and brush melted butter on top.
6. Bake for 17-20 minutes until golden and crispy.
7. Serve warm.

NUTRITIONAL VALUES (PER SERVING)
Calories: 330, Protein: 12g, Fat: 22g, Carbohydrates: 24g, Fiber: 3g, Sugar: 2g

FETA AND HERB STUFFED PEPPERS

INGREDIENTS

- 12 mini bell peppers, halved and seeded
- 1 cup feta cheese, crumbled
- 1/4 cup cream cheese, softened
- 1/4 cup fresh parsley, chopped
- 1/4 cup fresh mint, chopped
- 2 cloves garlic, minced
- Salt and pepper to taste
- Olive oil for drizzling

Prep Time: 15 Min
Cook Time: 10 Min

Servings: 4

DIRECTIONS

1. Instructions:
2. Preheat oven to 400°F (200°C). Arrange the baking sheet with parchment paper.
3. Mix feta cheese, cream cheese, parsley, mint, garlic, salt, and pepper in a bowl.
4. Stuff each bell pepper half with the cheese mixture and place on the parchment paper-arranged baking sheet.
5. Drizzle the stuffed peppers with olive oil and bake for 10 minutes.
6. Serve warm as a delightful snack or appetizer.

NUTRITIONAL VALUES (PER SERVING)
Calories: 220, Protein: 9g, Fat: 17g, Carbohydrates: 10g, Fiber: 2g, Sugar: 6g

GRILLED HALLOUMI CHEESE SKEWERS

INGREDIENTS

- 1 lb halloumi cheese, cut into 1-inch cubes
- 2 bell peppers, cut into pieces
- 1 zucchini, sliced into 1/2 inch thick rounds
- 1 red onion, cut into wedges
- 2 tablespoons olive oil
- 1 tablespoon lemon juice
- 1 teaspoon dried oregano
- Salt and crushed pepper to taste
- Wooden or metal skewers (if there are wooden, soak them in water for 30 minutes)

Prep Time: 15 Min
Cook Time: 10 Min

Servings: 4

DIRECTIONS

1. Preheat your grill to medium-high heat.
2. Combine the halloumi, bell peppers, zucchini, and red onion in a large bowl. Drizzle with olive oil and lemon juice. Powder it with oregano, salt, and pepper. Toss to coat evenly.
3. Thread the halloumi and vegetables alternately onto skewers.
4. Grill the skewers, turning occasionally, for about 8-10 minutes or until the vegetables are tender and the halloumi has grill marks.
5. Serve hot, garnished with additional lemon juice and fresh herbs if desired.

NUTRITIONAL VALUES (PER SERVING)
Calories: 380, Protein: 25g, Fat: 27g, Carbohydrates: 12g, Fiber: 2g, Sugar: 5g

MEDITERRANEAN BRUSCHETTA WITH TOMATO, BASIL, AND FETA

INGREDIENTS

- 1 baguette, sliced into 1/2-inch thick rounds
- 2 tablespoons olive oil
- 2 large tomatoes, diced
- 1/2 cup feta cheese, crumbled
- 1/4 cup fresh basil leaves, chopped
- 1 clove garlic, minced
- Salt and pepper to taste
- Balsamic glaze for drizzling (optional)

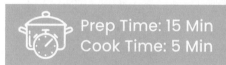 Prep Time: 15 Min
Cook Time: 5 Min

 Servings: 4

DIRECTIONS

1. Preheat oven to 400°F (200°C). Place the baguette slices on the oil-greased baking sheet and brush each with olive oil. Toast in the oven for 5 minutes.
2. Mix diced tomatoes, feta cheese, basil, garlic, salt, and pepper in a bowl.
3. Spread the tomato mixture onto the toasted baguette pieces. Drizzle with balsamic glaze if using.
4. Serve immediately, offering a fresh and flavorful appetizer or snack.

NUTRITIONAL VALUES (PER SERVING)
Calories: 290, Protein: 9g, Fat: 14g, Carbohydrates: 32g, Fiber: 2g, Sugar: 4g

ROASTED RED PEPPER AND WALNUT DIP (MUHAMMARA)

INGREDIENTS

- 2 cups roasted red peppers, drained
- 1 cup walnuts, toasted
- 1/2 cup breadcrumbs
- 2 tablespoons olive oil
- 1 tablespoon pomegranate molasses
- 1 teaspoon ground cumin
- 1/2 teaspoon smoked paprika
- Salt to taste
- 1 clove garlic, minced

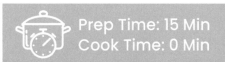

Prep Time: 15 Min
Cook Time: 0 Min

Servings: 4

DIRECTIONS

1. Combine roasted red peppers, walnuts, breadcrumbs, olive oil, pomegranate molasses, cumin, smoked paprika, salt, and garlic in a food processor. Process until smooth.
2. Taste and adjust the seasoning if necessary.
3. Transfer the dip to a serving bowl and chill in the refrigerator for at least 30 minutes to allow the flavors to meld.
4. Drizzle olive oil and serve with fresh vegetables or pita bread for dipping.

NUTRITIONAL VALUES (PER SERVING)

Calories: 330, Protein: 7g, Fat: 26g, Carbohydrates: 18g, Fiber: 4g, Sugar: 6g

GREEK YOGURT DIP WITH CUCUMBER AND DILL (TZATZIKI)

INGREDIENTS

- 1 cup Greek yogurt
- 1/2 cucumber, finely grated and drained
- 2 cloves garlic, minced
- 2 tablespoons fresh dill, chopped
- 1 tablespoon lemon juice
- Salt and pepper, to taste
- Olive oil, for drizzling

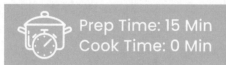 Prep Time: 15 Min
Cook Time: 0 Min

 Servings: 4

DIRECTIONS

1. Toss the Greek yogurt with grated cucumber, minced garlic, dill, and lemon juice in a shallow bowl. Stir well to combine.
2. Powder it with salt and pepper to taste. Drizzle olive oil (just a bit) before serving.
3. Serve chilled as a dip for vegetables and pita chips.

NUTRITIONAL VALUES (PER SERVING)
Calories: 70, Protein: 6g, Fat: 3g, Carbohydrates: 5g, Fiber: 0g, Sugar: 4g

CAPER BERRY AND CREAM CHEESE BITES

INGREDIENTS

- 8 oz cream cheese, softened
- 1/4 cup caper berries, drained and chopped
- 2 tablespoons chives, finely chopped
- Black pepper, to taste
- 1 baguette, sliced into rounds and toasted

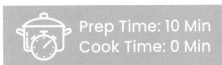 Prep Time: 10 Min
Cook Time: 0 Min

 Servings: 4

DIRECTIONS

1. Mix the cream cheese, chopped caper berries, and chives in a small bowl until well combined. Powder it with black pepper to taste.
2. Spread cream cheese mixture (a generous amount) onto each toasted baguette round.
3. Serve immediately as a flavorful and easy appetizer.

NUTRITIONAL VALUES (PER SERVING)
Calories: 290, Protein: 6g, Fat: 22g, Carbohydrates: 18g, Fiber: 1g, Sugar: 3g

MINI LAMB KEBABS WITH YOGURT SAUCE

INGREDIENTS

- For the Kebabs:
- 1 lb lamb, cut into 1-inch cubes
- 2 tablespoons olive oil
- 1 teaspoon ground cumin
- 1/2 teaspoon paprika
- Salt and pepper, to taste
- For the Yogurt Sauce:
- 1 cup Greek yogurt
- 1 clove garlic, minced
- 2 tablespoons fresh mint, chopped
- Salt and pepper, to taste
- Wooden or metal skewers

Prep Time: 25 Min
Cook Time: 10 Min

Servings: 4

DIRECTIONS

1. In a shallow bowl, combine lamb cubes with olive oil, cumin, paprika, salt, and pepper. Marinate for one hour (at least in the fridge).
2. Preheat a grill to medium-high heat.
3. Thread the marinated lamb onto skewers.
4. Grill the kebabs, turning occasionally, until browned and cooked to your liking, about 6-8 minutes for medium-rare.
5. For the yogurt sauce, mix Greek yogurt with garlic, mint, salt, and pepper in a shallow bowl.
6. Serve the lamb kebabs with the yogurt sauce on the side.

NUTRITIONAL VALUES (PER SERVING)

Calories: 350, Protein: 25g, Fat: 25g, Carbohydrates: 5g, Fiber: 0g, Sugar: 3g

BRUSCHETTA AL POMODORO

INGREDIENTS

- 4 large ripe tomatoes, diced
- 1/4 cup fresh basil leaves, chopped
- 2 cloves garlic, minced, plus 1 whole clove for rubbing
- 2 tablespoons extra virgin olive oil
- Salt and crushed black pepper, to taste
- 1 baguette, sliced into 1/2-inch thick rounds
- Balsamic glaze, for drizzling (optional)

Prep Time: 15 Min
Cook Time: 5 Min

Servings: 4

DIRECTIONS

1. Combine diced tomatoes, chopped basil, minced garlic, two tbsp oil, salt, and pepper in a shallow bowl. Stir to mix well. Let sit for 15 minutes to marinate.
2. Preheat your grill or broiler to high. Brush baguette slices lightly with olive oil. Grill or broil until golden and slightly crispy, about 1-2 minutes per side.
3. Rub the toasted baguette slices with a whole garlic clove for added flavor.
4. Top each bread slice with a generous spoonful of the tomato mixture.
5. Drizzle olive oil (just a bit) and balsamic glaze if using. Serve immediately.

NUTRITIONAL VALUES (PER SERVING)

Calories: 220, Protein: 6g, Fat: 10g, Carbohydrates: 28g, Fiber: 2g, Sugar: 4g

GREEK SPANAKOPITA

INGREDIENTS

- 1/2 lb fresh spinach, chopped and steamed
- 1 cup feta cheese, crumbled
- 1/4 cup onions, finely chopped
- 2 tablespoons dill, chopped
- 2 eggs, beaten
- Salt and pepper, to taste
- 1/4 cup olive oil
- 8 sheets of phyllo dough, thawed

Prep Time: 30 Min
Cook Time: 20 Min

Servings: 4

DIRECTIONS

1. Preheat oven to 375°F (190°C). Squeeze out excess water from the spinach.
2. Combine the spinach, feta cheese, onions, dill, and eggs in a shallow bowl. Season with salt and pepper.
3. Lay one phyllo sheet on a clean surface, brushing lightly with olive oil. Place another sheet on top and brush with oil. Cut the layered sheets into four strips.
4. Place a small amount of the spinach mixture at one end of every strip. Fold the excess phyllo sheet over the filling to form a triangle, continuing to fold in a triangle pattern until the strip is used up.
5. Place on a baking sheet. Brush the tops with more olive oil.
6. Bake for 17-20 minutes until golden and crispy. Serve warm.

NUTRITIONAL VALUES (PER SERVING)
Calories: 320, Protein: 12g, Fat: 20g, Carbohydrates: 24g, Fiber: 3g, Sugar: 3g

Vegetable Recipes

VEGAN PAELLA

 Prep Time: 20 Min
Cook Time: 40 Min

 Servings: 4

INGREDIENTS

- 2 tablespoons olive oil
- 1 onion, chopped
- 2 cloves garlic, minced
- 1 red bell pepper, sliced
- 1 yellow bell pepper, sliced
- 1 cup short-grain rice, such as Arborio or Calasparra
- 1/4 teaspoon saffron threads, crushed
- 1/2 teaspoon smoked paprika
- 3 cups vegetable broth
- 1 cup green peas, fresh or frozen
- 1 can (14 oz) artichoke hearts, drained and quartered
- 1/2 cup cherry tomatoes, halved
- Optional: 1 cup vegan sausage, sliced, or 1 cup tofu, cubed
- Salt and pepper to taste
- Lemon wedges, for serving
- Fresh parsley, chopped, for garnish

DIRECTIONS

1. Heat two tbsp oil in a large skillet or paella pan over medium heat. Add diced onion and mashed garlic, and sauté until softened.
2. Add bell peppers and saute for 2-3 minutes until slightly softened.
3. Toss in the rice, saffron, and smoked paprika until well coated.
4. Pour in the vegetable broth, boil, then reduce heat to a simmer. Arrange the peas, artichoke hearts, cherry tomatoes, and vegan sausage or tofu (if using) on top of the rice. Powder it with salt and pepper.
5. Cover and cook for 33-35 minutes until the rice is tender. Avoid stirring to prevent a crust from forming on the bottom.
6. Remove from heat and put it aside, covered, for 4-5 minutes.
7. Serve the paella garnished with lemon wedges and chopped parsley.

NUTRITIONAL VALUES (PER SERVING)
Calories: 350, Protein: 10g, Fat: 8g, Carbohydrates: 60g, Fiber: 8g, Sugar: 6g

MOROCCAN VEGETABLE TAGINE

INGREDIENTS

- 2 tablespoons olive oil
- 1 onion, chopped
- 2 cloves garlic, minced
- 2 carrots, peeled and sliced
- 2 potatoes, peeled and cubed
- 1 zucchini, sliced
- 1 can (15 oz weight) chickpeas, drained and rinsed
- 1 can (14 oz) diced tomatoes
- 3 cups vegetable broth
- 1 teaspoon ground cumin
- 1 teaspoon ground cinnamon
- 1/2 teaspoon ground ginger
- Salt and pepper to taste
- Fresh cilantro, for garnish
- Cooked couscous or rice, for serving

Prep Time: 15 Min
Cook Time: 60 Min

Servings: 4-6

DIRECTIONS

1. Heat two tbsp oil in a large pot or tagine over medium heat. Add diced onion and mashed garlic, and cook until softened.
2. Add carrots, potatoes, and zucchini to the pot. Cook for a few minutes until slightly softened.
3. Toss in chickpeas, diced tomatoes (with their juice), vegetable broth, cumin, cinnamon, and ginger. Powder it with salt and pepper.
4. Take this mixture to a boil, then decrease the stove heat, cover, and simmer for 45-60 minutes.
5. Serve the tagine over cooked couscous or rice, garnished with fresh cilantro.

NUTRITIONAL VALUES (PER SERVING)

Calories: 290, Protein: 9g, Fat: 7g, Carbohydrates: 50g, Fiber: 10g, Sugar: 9g

AUBERGINE (EGGPLANT) AND CHICKPEA CURRY

INGREDIENTS

- 2 tablespoons olive oil
- 1 large eggplant, cut into 1-inch cubes
- 1 onion, finely chopped
- 3 cloves garlic, minced
- 1 tablespoon ginger, grated
- 1 can (14 oz weight) chickpeas, drained and rinsed
- 1 can (14 oz) diced tomatoes
- 1 can (14 oz) coconut milk
- 2 teaspoons curry powder
- 1 teaspoon ground cumin
- 1/2 teaspoon ground turmeric
- Salt and pepper to taste
- Cooked rice or flatbread, for serving
- Fresh cilantro, for garnish

 Prep Time: 15 Min
Cook Time: 40 Min

 Servings: 4

DIRECTIONS

1. Heat two tbsp oil in a large skillet over medium heat. Add eggplant wedges and cook until they soften and brown, about 10 minutes. Remove from the skillet and set aside.
2. Add diced onion, mashed garlic, and ginger to the same skillet. Cook for 5 minutes.
3. Toss in the chickpeas, diced tomatoes, coconut milk, curry powder, cumin, and turmeric. Powder it with salt and pepper.
4. Return the eggplant to the skillet. Bring to a simmer, then decrease the stove heat and cook for 21-25 minutes, or until the curry is thickened and the eggplant is tender.
5. Serve the curry over cooked rice or flatbread, garnished with fresh cilantro.

NUTRITIONAL VALUES (PER SERVING)
Calories: 350, Protein: 9g, Fat: 18g, Carbohydrates: 42g, Fiber: 12g, Sugar: 14g

CANNELLINI BEAN STEW WITH TOMATOES AND KALE

INGREDIENTS

- 2 tablespoons olive oil
- 1 onion, chopped
- 2 cloves garlic, minced
- 1 can (14 oz) cannellini beans, drained and rinsed
- 1 can (14 oz) diced tomatoes
- 4 cups kale, chopped
- 2 cups vegetable broth
- 1 teaspoon dried thyme
- Salt and pepper to taste
- 1 piece of crusty bread, to serve
- Grated vegan Parmesan cheese, for garnish (optional)

 Prep Time: 10 Min
Cook Time: 30 Min

 Servings: 4

DIRECTIONS

1. Heat two tbsp oil in a large pot over medium heat. Add diced onion, mashed garlic, and sauté until the onion is soft, about 5 minutes.
2. Add the cannellini beans, diced tomatoes (with their juice), kale, vegetable broth, and thyme. Powder it with salt and pepper.
3. Bring to a boil, then decrease the stove heat and simmer for about 20 minutes, or until the kale is tender and the stew has thickened.
4. Serve hot with rusty bread on the side. Garnish with grated vegan Parmesan cheese if desired.

NUTRITIONAL VALUES (PER SERVING)
Calories: 250, Protein: 10g, Fat: 7g, Carbohydrates: 37g, Fiber: 10g, Sugar: 6g

PASTA ALLA NORMA (VEGAN VERSION)

INGREDIENTS

- 1 lb pasta (rigatoni or penne)
- 1/4 cup olive oil
- 1 large eggplant, cubed
- Salt to taste
- 1 onion, chopped
- 2 cloves garlic, minced
- 1 can (28 oz) crushed tomatoes
- 1 teaspoon dried oregano
- Fresh basil leaves for garnish
- Vegan Parmesan cheese for serving

Prep Time: 20 Min
Cook Time: 30 Min

Servings: 4

DIRECTIONS

1. Prepare pasta as per packet steps until al dente. Drain and set aside.
2. Meanwhile, heat one-fourth of the oil in a large skillet over medium heat. Add eggplant cubes, season with salt, and cook until golden and soft, about 10 minutes. Remove from the skillet and set aside.
3. Add diced onion and mashed garlic in the same skillet, cooking until the onion is translucent, about 5 minutes.
4. Toss in the crushed tomatoes and oregano. Bring to a simmer and cook for 11-15 minutes or until the sauce has thickened.
5. Return the cooked eggplant and mix well.
6. Toss the prepared pasta with the eggplant and tomato sauce. Serve garnished with fresh basil leaves and vegan Parmesan cheese.

NUTRITIONAL VALUES (PER SERVING)

Calories: 510, Protein: 15g, Fat: 14g, Carbohydrates: 82g, Fiber: 11g, Sugar: 12g

CHICKPEA AND SPINACH STEW WITH SMOKED PAPRIKA

INGREDIENTS

- 2 tablespoons olive oil
- 1 onion, chopped
- 2 cloves garlic, minced
- 1 teaspoon smoked paprika
- 1 can (14 oz weight) chickpeas, drained and rinsed
- 1 can (14 oz) diced tomatoes
- 4 cups fresh spinach
- Salt and pepper to taste
- 1 cup vegetable broth
- Crusty bread, for serving

 Prep Time: 15 Min
Cook Time: 30 Min

 Servings: 4

DIRECTIONS

1. Heat two tbsp oil in a large pot over medium heat. Add diced onion and mashed garlic, cooking until softened, about 5 minutes.
2. Toss in the smoked paprika, chickpeas, and diced tomatoes. Cook for 5 minutes.
3. Add the spinach and vegetable broth. Season with salt and pepper. Cook the spinach for 7-10 minutes.
4. Serve the stew hot, accompanied by crusty bread for dipping.

NUTRITIONAL VALUES (PER SERVING)

Calories: 250, Protein: 9g, Fat: 8g, Carbohydrates: 36g, Fiber: 9g, Sugar: 7g

BAKED RATATOUILLE

INGREDIENTS

- 1 zucchini, thinly sliced
- 1 eggplant, thinly sliced
- 1 red bell pepper, thinly sliced
- 1 yellow bell pepper, thinly sliced
- 2 cups tomato sauce
- 2 cloves garlic, minced
- 1 teaspoon dried thyme
- Salt and pepper to taste
- Olive oil, for drizzling
- Fresh basil, for garnish
- Crusty bread, for serving

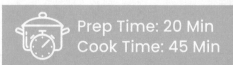

Prep Time: 20 Min
Cook Time: 45 Min

Servings: 4

DIRECTIONS

1. Preheat oven to 375°F (190°C). Spread tomato sauce in the baking dish. Sprinkle with minced garlic and thyme.
2. Arrange the slices of zucchini, eggplant, and bell peppers in alternating layers on top of the sauce. Powder it with salt and pepper, and drizzle with olive oil.
3. Cover the dish and bake for 31-35 minutes. Uncover and bake more for 10 minutes or until the vegetables are tender.
4. Garnish with fresh basil before serving. Serve with crusty bread on the side.

NUTRITIONAL VALUES (PER SERVING)

Calories: 180, Protein: 5g, Fat: 5g, Carbohydrates: 30g, Fiber: 9g, Sugar: 13g

BUTTERNUT SQUASH AND SAGE RISOTTO

INGREDIENTS

- 1 cup arborio rice
- 2 tablespoons olive oil
- 1 butternut squash small size, peeled, seeded, and cubed
- 1 onion, chopped
- 2 cloves garlic, minced
- 4 cups vegetable broth, warmed
- 1/2 cup white wine (optional)
- 2 tablespoons fresh sage, chopped
- Salt and pepper to taste
- 1/4 cup nutritional yeast

Prep Time: 15 Min
Cook Time: 30 Min

Servings: 4

DIRECTIONS

1. Preheat oven to 400°F (200°C). Toss the butternut squash cubes with one tbsp oil, salt, and crushed pepper. Roast for 25 minutes or until tender.
2. In a large pan, heat the leftover olive oil over medium heat. Add diced onion and mashed garlic, cooking until the onion is translucent.
3. Toss in the arborio rice, coating it in the oil. If using, ladle in the white wine and stir until mostly absorbed.
4. Add vegetable broth, and keep stirring one cup/ladle at a time. Wait until each addition is almost fully absorbed before adding the next.
5. When the rice is creamy and just tender, Toss in the roasted butternut squash, sage, and nutritional yeast. Season with salt and pepper to taste.
6. Serve the risotto warm, garnished with additional sage if desired.

NUTRITIONAL VALUES (PER SERVING)

Calories: 350, Protein: 10g, Fat: 10g, Carbohydrates: 55g, Fiber: 5g, Sugar: 4g

CAULIFLOWER AND POTATO CURRY

INGREDIENTS

- 2 tablespoons vegetable oil
- 1 onion, finely chopped
- 2 cloves garlic, minced
- 1 tablespoon ginger, grated
- 1 tablespoon curry powder
- 1 teaspoon ground turmeric
- 1/2 teaspoon ground cumin
- 1 cauliflower, cut into florets
- 2 potatoes, peeled and cubed
- 1 can (14 oz) coconut milk
- 1 cup vegetable broth
- Salt and pepper to taste
- Fresh cilantro, for garnish

 Prep Time: 15 Min
Cook Time: 30 Min

 Servings: 4

DIRECTIONS

1. Heat two tbsp oil in a large pot over medium heat. Add diced onion, mashed garlic, and ginger, sautéing until the onion is translucent.
2. Toss in the curry powder, turmeric, and cumin, cooking for 1 minute until fragrant.
3. Add the cauliflower florets and potato cubes, stirring to coat them in the spices.
4. Ladle in the coconut milk and vegetable broth. Season with salt and pepper.
5. Bring to a boil, then decrease the stove heat and simmer; keep it covered for 21-25 minutes or until the vegetables are tender.
6. Garnish with fresh cilantro before serving. This curry is delicious served over rice or with naan bread.

NUTRITIONAL VALUES (PER SERVING)
Calories: 350, Protein: 6g, Fat: 22g, Carbohydrates: 34g, Fiber: 6g, Sugar: 6g

VEGETABLE WHITE RICE

INGREDIENTS

- 2 cups white rice
- 4 cups water
- 2 tablespoons olive oil
- 1/2 cup green beans, trimmed and chopped
- 1/2 cup green peas
- 1/2 cup diced carrot
- 1/2 cup cauliflower florets
- Salt and pepper to taste

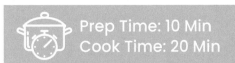

Prep Time: 10 Min
Cook Time: 20 Min

Servings: 4

DIRECTIONS

1. Make sure the rice is thoroughly cleaned by running cold water over it. Make sure to drain well.
2. Heat the water in a big pot until it boils. Lower the heat to low and add the rice and a small salt pinch. After the water has been absorbed
3. and the rice is soft, cook it covered for 15 to 18 minutes.
4. In a skillet over medium heat, warm the olive oil while the rice cooks.
5. Add the green beans, green peas, diced carrot, and cauliflower florets. Sauté until the vegetables are just tender, about 5-7 minutes. Season with salt and pepper.
6. Once the rice is done, fluff it and gently mix in the sautéed vegetables.
7. Serve the vegetable white rice as a side dish or enjoy it as a light main course. It pairs well with a variety of dishes and offers a simple, nutritious option for any meal.

NUTRITIONAL VALUES (PER SERVING)

Calories: 310, Protein: 6g, Fat: 7g, Carbohydrates: 55g, Fiber: 3g, Sugar: 3g

Low-sugar Dessert Recipes

GRILLED PEACHES WITH PISTACHIOS

INGREDIENTS

- 4 ripe peaches, halved and pitted
- 1 tablespoon olive oil
- 1/4 cup pistachios, crushed
- Optional: Honey or a drizzle of balsamic glaze for serving

 Prep Time: 10 Min
Cook Time: 8 Min

 Servings: 4

DIRECTIONS

1. Set your grill's temperature to medium-high.
2. Apply olive oil (a thin layer) to the peaches' sliced sides.
3. Lay the peaches on the grill and cut the side down. Grill the peaches for 4–5 minutes, or until
4. they begin to soften and develop grill marks.
5.
6. After flipping the peaches, grill them for a further three to four minutes.
7. Take it off the grill and give it a little cooling time.
8. Sprinkle the grilled peaches with crushed pistachios. If desired, drizzle with honey or balsamic glaze for added sweetness.
9. Serve warm as a delightful, low-sugar dessert that's both simple and sophisticated.

NUTRITIONAL VALUES (PER SERVING)

Calories: 120, Protein: 2g, Fat: 7g, Carbohydrates: 14g, Fiber: 3g, Sugar: 11g (without honey or glaze)

ALMOND STUFFED DATES

INGREDIENTS

- 12 Medjool dates
- 12 whole almonds
- Optional: A pinch of sea salt or a sprinkle of cocoa powder for dusting

 Prep Time: 10 Min
Cook Time: 0 Min

 Servings: 4

DIRECTIONS

1. Slit each date on one side and remove the pit.
2. Insert a whole almond into the cavity of each date.
3. For an added flavor boost, feel free to dust the stuffed dates with a little cocoa powder or a tiny pinch of sea salt.
4. Serve immediately or, for a refreshing treat, chill in the fridge before serving.
5. These almond-stuffed dates offer a naturally sweet taste with a satisfying crunch, making them a perfect healthy dessert or snack.

NUTRITIONAL VALUES (PER SERVING)

Calories: 180, Protein: 2g, Fat: 4g, Carbohydrates: 36g, Fiber: 4g, Sugar: 32g

CUCUMBER AND WATERMELON GAZPACHO

INGREDIENTS

- 2 cups cubed watermelon
- 1 large cucumber, peeled and cubed
- 1/4 cup fresh mint leaves
- Juice of 1 lime
- 1 tablespoon honey (optional, for a slightly sweeter taste)
- Pinch of salt

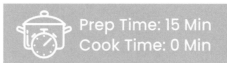 Prep Time: 15 Min
Cook Time: 0 Min

 Servings: 4

DIRECTIONS

1. In the high-power blender, combine the watermelon, cucumber, mint leaves, lime juice, honey (if using), and a pinch of salt. Blend until smooth.
2. Taste and adjust the seasoning if necessary.
3. Chill the gazpacho for one hour before serving.
4. Serve the gazpacho cold, garnished with additional mint leaves or cucumber slices.

NUTRITIONAL VALUES (PER SERVING)

Calories: 50, Protein: 1g, Fat: 0g, Carbohydrates: 12g, Fiber: 1g, Sugar: 10g (with optional honey)

AVOCADO CHOCOLATE MOUSSE

INGREDIENTS

- 2 ripe avocados, pitted and scooped
- 1/4 cup cocoa powder
- 1/4 cup honey or maple syrup
- 1 teaspoon vanilla extract
- A pinch of salt
- Fresh raspberries or mint leaves for garnish (optional)

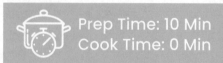

Prep Time: 10 Min
Cook Time: 0 Min

Servings: 4

DIRECTIONS

1. Add avocado, cocoa powder, honey or maple syrup, vanilla extract, and salt in the high-power food processor. Blend until smooth and creamy.
2. Taste and adjust the sweetness if necessary. Divide the mousse and chill for at least 1 hour to set.
3. Garnish with fresh raspberries or mint leaves before serving, if desired. Enjoy a rich and creamy dessert that's delicious and packed with healthy fats and nutrients.

NUTRITIONAL VALUES (PER SERVING)

Calories: 230, Protein: 3g, Fat: 15g, Carbohydrates: 28g, Fiber: 7g, Sugar: 17g

ZUCCHINI AND LEMON CAKE

INGREDIENTS

- 2 cups almond flour
- 1/2 cup sweetener of choice (erythritol for lower sugar content)
- 2 teaspoons baking powder
- 1/2 teaspoon salt
- 2 cups grated zucchini, squeezed to remove excess moisture
- 3 large eggs
- 1/4 cup olive oil
- Zest and juice of 1 lemon
- 1 teaspoon vanilla extract

Prep Time: 20 Min
Cook Time: 45 Min

Servings: 8

DIRECTIONS

1. Preheat oven to 350°F (175°C). Grease and arrange the loaf pan with parchment paper. Toss the almond flour, sweetener, baking powder, and salt in the large, deep-bottom bowl.
2. Toss in the grated zucchini, eggs, olive oil, lemon zest, lemon juice, and vanilla extract .
3. Ladle the batter into the prepared loaf pan and smooth the top. Bake for 46-50 minutes until a toothstick inserted and comes out clean.
4. Let the cake cool, then transfer to the wire rack to cool completely.
5. Slice and serve the cake, enjoying the moist texture and refreshing lemon flavor.

NUTRITIONAL VALUES (PER SERVING)
Calories: 280, Protein: 9g, Fat: 23g, Carbohydrates: 14g, Fiber: 4g, Sugar: 5g

AVOCADO LIME ICE CREAM

INGREDIENTS

- 2 ripe avocados
- 1/2 cup coconut milk
- 1/4 cup lime juice
- Zest of 2 limes
- 1/4 cup honey or maple syrup
- A pinch of salt

 Prep Time: 10 Min
Cook Time: 0 Min

 Servings: 4

DIRECTIONS

1. Combine the avocados, coconut milk, lime juice, zest, honey or maple syrup, and salt (just a pinch) in the high-power blender. Blend until smooth and creamy.
2. Taste and adjust the sweetness or lime flavor if necessary.
3. Ladle the mixture into an ice cream maker and churn according to the manufacturer's instructions. Alternatively, freeze the mixture in a container, stirring every 30 minutes, until firm.
4. Once frozen to your desired consistency, scoop and serve the ice cream garnished with additional lime zest.
5. Enjoy a creamy and refreshing dessert that's perfect for a hot day or any occasion when you crave something sweet yet healthy.

NUTRITIONAL VALUES (PER SERVING)

Calories: 250, Protein: 3g, Fat: 18g, Carbohydrates: 22g, Fiber: 7g, Sugar: 12g

RICOTTA AND LEMON ZEST BALLS

INGREDIENTS

- 1 cup ricotta cheese
- Zest of 1 lemon
- 2 tablespoons erythritol or stevia, adjusted to taste
- Optional: Unsweetened coconut flakes or crushed almonds for coating

 Prep Time: 15 Min
Cook Time: 60 Min

 Servings: 4

DIRECTIONS

1. Combine the ricotta cheese, lemon zest, and erythritol or stevia in a mixing bowl. Mix well until fully incorporated.
2. Scoop out the mixture, then roll into balls with your hands.
3. If desired, roll the balls in unsweetened coconut flakes or crushed almonds to coat.
4. Place the balls on the parchment paper-arranged plate or tray and refrigerate for one hour until firm.
5. Serve chilled as a refreshing and light dessert option.

NUTRITIONAL VALUES (PER SERVING)

Calories: 100, Protein: 6g, Fat: 7g, Carbohydrates: 3g, Fiber: 0g, Sugar: 1g
(varies based on sweetener and coatings used)

ALMOND AND ORANGE FLOUR CAKE

INGREDIENTS

- 2 cups almond flour
- 1 cup orange flour (or finely ground dried orange peel mixed with almond flour)
- 1/2 cup erythritol or stevia, adjusted to taste
- 4 eggs
- 1/2 cup olive oil
- 1 teaspoon baking powder
- Zest of 1 orange
- Juice of 1 orange

 Prep Time: 20 Min
Cook Time: 35 Min

 Servings: 8

DIRECTIONS

1. Preheat oven to 350°F (175°C). Grease and flour a 9-inch cake pan.
2. Combine almond flour, orange flour, erythritol or stevia, and baking powder in the large, deep-bottom bowl.
3. In the other deep-bottom bowl, beat the eggs with the olive oil, orange zest, and orange juice until well mixed.
4. Combine the wet and dry elements, mixing until smooth.
5. Ladle the batter into the prepared cake pan and smooth the top.
6. Bake for 31-35 minutes until a tooth-stick inserted into the center comes out clean.
7. Let the cake cool.
8. Serve as is or with a dusting of erythritol or a drizzle of honey.

NUTRITIONAL VALUES (PER SERVING)

Calories: 320, Protein: 9g, Fat: 28g, Carbohydrates: 10g, Fiber: 4g, Sugar: 2g
(varies based on sweetener used)

DARK CHOCOLATE DIPPED STRAWBERRIES

INGREDIENTS

- 1-pint fresh strawberries, washed and dried
- 6 oz dark chocolate (70% cocoa or higher), chopped
- Optional: Stevia or erythritol, to taste, for sweeter chocolate

Prep Time: 15 Min
Cook Time: 30 Min

Servings: 4

DIRECTIONS

1. Arrange the baking sheet with parchment paper. In a microwave, melt the dark chocolate until smooth. Sweeten with stevia or erythritol if desired.
2. Holding them by the stem, dip the strawberries into the melted chocolate, turning to coat evenly. Place the dipped strawberries on the prepared baking sheet.
3. Refrigerate for at least 30 minutes until the chocolate is set.
4. Serve chilled as a delightful and simple dessert.

NUTRITIONAL VALUES (PER SERVING)

Calories: 200, Protein: 3g, Fat: 12g, Carbohydrates: 20g, Fiber: 5g, Sugar: 12g

PISTACHIO AND OLIVE OIL CAKE

INGREDIENTS

- 1 cup ground pistachios
- 1 cup all-purpose flour
- 1/2 cup olive oil
- 3/4 cup honey
- 3 eggs
- 1 teaspoon vanilla extract
- 1 teaspoon baking powder
- Pinch of salt
- Optional: Whole pistachios for garnish

Prep Time: 20 Min
Cook Time: 40 Min

Servings: 8

DIRECTIONS

1. Preheat oven to 350°F (175°C). Grease and flour a 9-inch cake pan.
2. Mix the ground pistachios, flour, baking powder, and salt
3. in the deep-bottom bowl.
4. Whisk the eggs, olive oil, honey, and vanilla extract in the other shallow bowl until well combined.
5. Gradually add the dry elements to the wet ingredients, stirring until just combined and without over-mixing.
6. Ladle the batter into the prepared cake pan and smooth the top with a spatula.
7. If desired, sprinkle whole pistachios over the top of the batter for garnish.
8. Bake for 40 minutes until a tooth-stick inserted and comes out clean.
9. Allow the cake to cool.
10. Once cooled, then serve with a light dusting of powdered sugar.

NUTRITIONAL VALUES (PER SERVING)
Calories: 380, Protein: 7g, Fat: 22g, Carbohydrates: 42g, Fiber: 2g, Sugar: 25g

Made in the USA
Columbia, SC
27 May 2024